Beyond Animal Rights
Food, Pets and Ethics

Tony Milligan

continuum

Continuum International Publishing Group

The Tower Building	80 Maiden Lane
11 York Road	Suite 704
London SE1 7NX	New York, NY 10038

www.continuumbooks.com

British Library Cataloguing-in-Publication Data
A catalogue record for this book is available from the British Library.

ISBN: HB: 978-1-4411-9486-2
      PB: 978-1-4411-5753-9

Library of Congress Cataloging-in-Publication Data
Milligan, Tony.
Beyond animal rights : food, pets, and ethics / Tony Milligan.
   p. cm.
Includes bibliographical references.
ISBN-13: 978-1-4411-9486-2
ISBN-10: 1-4411-9486-X
ISBN-13: 978-1-4411-5753-9 (pbk.)
ISBN-10: 1-4411-5753-0 (pbk.)
1. Animal rights. I. Title.

HV4708.M55 2010
179'.3–dc22   2010011664

Typeset by Newgen Imaging Systems Pvt Ltd, Chennai, India
Printed and bound in India by Replika Press Pvt Ltd

To Suzanne, who has been my guide.

Contents

Preface

For the foreseeable future, our human community will be a community of mixed eaters. Most of us will be carnivores, a significant minority will be vegetarians and a much smaller minority will be vegans (eating no meat, no eggs and no dairy produce). Where any one of us fits into this dietary patchwork will depend upon how we were brought up, whether we are ready to reconsider our dietary practices, and how we see these practices in the light of a variety of considerations, at least some of which will be personal or ethical or both. We may, for example, wonder about how to square meat-eating with the love that we have for our pets. For any one of us, reflection upon a single consideration can tip the balance but the ordinary pattern of our deliberation about diet is to factor in a variety of matters rather than restricting ourselves to one big claim.

I have tried to write in line with this familiar pattern of practical deliberation and not to appeal to any knock-down argument for or against animal rights. (A right not to be experimented upon, a right not to be eaten and so on.) This is not because I reject the idea of animal rights but because we are liable to miss a great deal if we appeal only, or primarily to rights. After all, we have a much richer body of ethical concepts at our disposal, concerning harm, cruelty, care, brutality, authority, suffering and well-being. These help us to fix our relations to each other and to other creatures. Unlike the language of rights, which is used intermittently, some of these concepts are in daily use; they are part of our everyday lives as ethical agents. And if I were writing more exclusively about humans I would still tend to use these concepts rather than focusing primarily or exclusively upon rights. A young woman being forced into a marriage by her parents might, after all, appeal to her rights but we would understand more about her predicament if she were to appeal to their cruelty or their uncaring attitude.

Rights claims and attributions can sometimes clarify matters, but they tend to make sense only against the backdrop of broader ways of relating to other humans and to other creatures, ways that are informed by the wider range of our ethical concepts. In the light of this statement, some philosophically trained readers may be tempted to classify this book as an exercise in what is known as virtue ethics. After all, some of our important ethical concepts concern the virtues and vices ('practical wisdom', 'cruelty', 'humility'; 'balance'; 'justice' and so on). While this may do no harm, it is not entirely the way in which I see matters. The reader who resists such a temptation or who lacks familiarity with the involved philosophical disputes between virtue ethics and rival theories (about rights and consequences) may be better able to understand my position.

For what it is worth, I regard the attempt to enshrine a single concept (rights, consequences, the Good, virtue) as sovereign over all moral deliberations as a hangover from monotheism. We do not need a sovereign concept, but we do need a rich ethical vocabulary. Again, for what it is worth, I happen to be a pluralist about ethics, and this I hope brings me closer to the best in our ordinary, familiar ways of deliberating about ethical matters. I draw upon a range of concepts some of which are recognizably virtue terms but some of which (such as 'suffering') are not. My own deliberations about ethics, about my personal situation and about the life that I share with my wife Suzanne have led me to adopt a vegan diet, although in earlier days I have been successively a carnivore and then a vegetarian. But I do not claim that everyone has the same reasons that I do to live as a vegan.

One of the attractions of pluralism about ethics is that it allows our actions to be constrained by a variety of reasons rather than reducing our deliberations down to a simple binary matter of deciding that everyone should do one thing or else that they (we) should all do the opposite. A problem with thinking about animals primarily in terms of a right not to be eaten is that it encourages just such an all or nothing approach. And this is difficult to reconcile with what we recognize as morally acceptable. It was, I think, clearly acceptable for our ancestors to eat meat and for hunter gatherers to go on doing so. It is an integral part of their life, a part of what makes them who they are. They have reasons for meat-eating that we do not have. Similarly, it is non-controversial that people in less prosperous parts of the world should eat whatever they need in order to give them their best chance of survival.

It may be more plausible to say that animals have a right not to be eaten by relatively affluent humans in Western countries such as the United States and the United Kingdom. But I think that this still misses something important. Smallholders in more prosperous countries, who have built a good and environmentally friendly way of life for themselves and for their families, clearly have reasons for meat-eating that I do not have and that most readers of this book will also not have. We may then adopt a reformulated claim and say that animals have a right not to be eaten without a good reason, and this may be closer to the mark, but it dilutes the idea of a right to the point where a claim of right looses much of its force.

What guides this book is instead the background idea of a scale of reasons. At one end of the scale, I would place hunter-gatherers; those whose nutritional requirements might not otherwise be met if they did not eat meat; those with medical conditions that make dietary change a dangerous risk (e.g. patients undergoing or recovering from chemotherapy); individuals with a history of anorexia who might unwittingly use a vegetarian or vegan diet to mask a recurrence of their condition; and those in a stage of later life whose habits are fixed, whose dietary range is limited, and whose health is precarious. A little further along this scale I would place ethically minded smallholders, and a little further still those who belong to communities that contain significant numbers of such smallholders.

At the other end of the scale, I would place most of the rest of us, and, in particular, healthy and reasonably well-off urbanites who lack any obvious and sufficient reasons for meat-eating. As for the reader, and where you should place yourself on such a scale, I do not know enough about your life to make an informed judgement. If it helps, I will say that my broader view is that most of us probably do not have enough good reasons to continue to eat meat and none of us has good enough reasons to eat meat produced through cruel systems of industrial farming. The fact that we tolerate such systems may also lead us to question whether we have lost moral authority in other areas, in particular with regard to animal experimentation for serious purposes. I will suggest that, as matters stand, we probably have lost this authority.

None of this should be taken to imply that those who eat meat without sufficient reasons for doing so should be regarded as callous or (as one critic suggests) gluttonous. Some of them may be, but I suspect that they are the exception. This book opens with an attempt to show that, for the most part, such meat-eaters mistakenly believe themselves to have deep reasons for their dietary practice. But, for most of us, meat-eating is not and never has been a deep part of our lives. To be mistaken in this way about what is deep and what is not is no special distinction that marks out meat-eaters from non meat-eaters. It is simply part of being human and therefore liable to be mistaken about many things on a large number of occasions. What is unfortunate about mistakes in this context is that widespread meat-eating requires so many victims and so much suffering.

1 The Depth of Meat-Eating

ARGUMENTS AND BACKGROUND PICTURES

There is a familiar style of setting out the arguments for and against vegetarianism which involves considering a series of standard claims and counter-claims to legitimate and guide our actions. So, for example, the meat-eater may say that animals caught up in the food chain need not suffer unduly, and the vegetarian may reply by claiming that industrial food production makes cruel forms of suffering unavoidable. The vegetarian may go on to point out that loss of sentient life is a morally troubling form of harm that is suffered even if it is not experienced. Harm and the awareness of harm can be two different things. The meat-eater may respond by pointing out that without breeding for human (and pet) consumption a great many animals would not be alive at all. And so the discussion goes.

If a convincing intellectual case is then made for vegetarianism, and neither party to the discussion is just plain stubborn, then as reasonable agents it may be expected that both parties will abjure the flesh of other creatures. Or so we might expect. There are even some literary accounts of the conversion of individuals to vegetarianism that fit this picture very well. Peter Singer, who is the best-known advocate of 'animal liberation', has tried repeatedly to defuse any charge that his own position is sentimentally motivated by emphasizing that he has never had any particular fondness for animals. Recalling a research visit with his wife to a self-professed lover of animals, he describes the uphill task of outlining his position, 'We didn't "love" animals. We simply wanted them treated as the independent sentient beings that they are, and not as a means to human ends-as the pig whose flesh was now in our hostess's sandwiches had been treated.'[1] Singer stresses that his own vegetarianism flows out of intellectual conviction, out of his having been convinced pretty much in the manner described above.

This is an impressive example of being willing to go wherever the arguments take us. But more often a strong case for vegetarianism may have little motivating force. The example and perplexity of another philosopher, Stephen Law, may be more characteristic. Stephen is the author of a number of popular introductions to philosophy, two of which include brief accounts of the pros and cons of meat-eating. He concludes one of these accounts by noting that 'I eat meat. But I have to admit, I find the moral arguments for not eating meat to be very powerful.'[2] The other account ends on a similarly strained note, 'Many of us think it is "just obvious" that it's morally acceptable to kill and eat other species of animal. I did until I started reading philosophy. But I'm now finding it increasingly difficult to defend my meat-eating lifestyle.'[3]

I take it that this predicament is more characteristic than Peter Singer's conversion. It is a curious feature of the familiar arguments for vegetarianism that their merit can be appreciated by those who do not go on to change their lives. A general philosophical explanation for this may be given, one that considers the merits of *motivational judgment internalism*: the view that holding some action to be the right thing to do is inseparable from having at least some motivation to carry it out.[4] The existence of carnivores who appreciate and even accept the case for vegetarianism, in the abstract, may suggest that *motivational judgment internalism* is a mistaken position to hold. If, instead, there is no connection between making judgments and being motivated, then we can readily understand why a winning argument for vegetarianism can still remain an ineffective argument.

A disadvantage of this explanation is that there often does seem to be some connection between our moral judgments and the way that we are inclined to act. What is striking about the frequent ineffectiveness of the case for vegetarianism is that its failure to motivate seems anomalous. It is *not* what normally happens. For example, when we realize that global warming is a serious problem we try to do something about it, even if our efforts do not match the scale of the problem. The absence of a change in lifestyle by some of those who believe that vegetarianism is perhaps the best option may prompt a more misanthropic appraisal. We may begin to suspect that people are ultimately selfish, or callous or just plain lazy. It would then be easy to understand why any slight motivation that is provided by the arguments might be trumped or overwhelmed by dietary convenience and an unwillingness to change. This may be part of what Elizabeth Telfer has in mind when she suggests that 'a common reason for failure to respect animal rights is not lack of belief in the animals' cause, but simply gluttony.' Telfer backs up this rather harsh assessment with an instructive anecdote, recalling an occasion when she said to a friend, 'You know, I can't help thinking that there is something in the arguments in favour of vegetarianism.' 'Of course there is', she replied, 'but meat's nice.'[5] Here we might connect up gluttony to lust, not in the sense of a healthy sexual desire but of allowing our desires to run riot irrespective of the harm to others. The expense or cost in terms of harm and animal lives may seem great when weighed against the apparent triviality of any stated reason for meat-eating (the pleasures of taste, of smell, of familiar forms of conviviality and so on).

This misanthropic assessment can be resisted. We may, more generously, allow, as Peter Singer does, that humans are subject to personal inertia. We are individually and *en masse*, locked into our habits and this is part of the reason why a simple conversion by argument can often be ineffective. He describes our habits as 'the final barrier that the Animal Liberation movement faces. Habits not only of diet but of thought and language must be challenged and altered'.[6] And this is part of the story, but perhaps not all of it. Others philosophers, such as Cora Diamond, have pointed out that philosophical argument cannot be left to do all the work of practical reason.[7] We also need to be able to picture life in realistic and imaginative ways, and such picturing may have a complex relation to the arguments that we accept and supply. On such a view, the convincing and effective advocate of vegetarianism, the one who makes an impact upon the world, needs not only argument but realistic ways of picturing the merits of their own way of living and the tensions involved in any altern-ative. Advocates of meat-eating do not need to learn this lesson. Representing matters favourably is something that they have always done well. Their practice, and commitment to argue in its defence, draws in many cases upon a background picture of what an authentic, truthful or *natural* human life has to be like. This background picture may be more impressive than some of the arguments advanced to support it. I want to suggest that the vegetarian can and ought to challenge the background picture, but this will involve a combination of argument and of representing (picturing) what it is to live well.

MEAT-EATING AND WELL-BEING

Just what the defender of meat-eating appeals to, and what the vegetarian needs to challenge, can be difficult to explain. To make headway, I will call upon a story set out in a vegan cookbook by Tanya Bernard and Sarah Kramer, *How it all Vegan*. One of its co-authors, Tanya Bernard, describes her carnivorous upbringing in the following terms,

> I grew up in a household where it was believed that 'meat is the fuel that keeps bodies healthy and strong'. My father was an adamant

meat-eater; he loved the stuff. Throughout my formative years, he would always say to me, 'We have to eat at least two servings of meat daily'. I never questioned this.[8]

The claim would be questioned now, and this might lead us to imagine that all Tanya learnt when she grew up and stopped eating meat was dietary information about how healthy the vegetarian or vegan alternative can be. We might suspect that her father was just badly informed and there is an end to the matter.

What we can miss by moving so quickly to judgment is that Tanya's father may have been attempting to articulate something more than dietary information. He may be read as someone who assumed that there is more to eating-well than nutrition, and that meat-eating is part and parcel of an all-round healthy life for a human, a life that is healthy in more than a strictly medical sense. He may be read, generously, as someone who was trying to represent meat-eating as a practice that is in some way *deep* and more particularly a practice that is deeply connected to our own well-being.

That meat-eating is a deep practice is, in one sense, obviously true. It is deeply entangled with our existing food chains, our farming practices, with commerce, trade, socialization, celebrations and rituals (most of which involve celebratory meals) and even with our infantile introduction to the world of eating solids. The practice is deep in a way that separates it out from more recent innovations, such as fox hunting, routine animal experimentation and dog shows. It is at the core of our ways of relating to animals, it has much stronger historical roots than any of the above and it would be commensurately harder for an entire society to abandon. On this basis, it is difficult to envisage a situation in which meat-eating would actually be outlawed. Vegetarian and vegan literature tends to make no such call and appeals instead to informed personal choice. A vegan pamphlet, before me as I write, calls upon its readers to 'choose to be kinder to animals'.[9] A distant situation in which an entire society voluntarily abandoned the practice of meat-eating may also strike us as so unlikely that it would involve an effectively impossible scenario, or at least one that is on a par with the farther reaches of science fiction. The practice of meat-eating is, admittedly, deep in this way, although deeply embedded practices have, from time to time, been at least partially uprooted. Sexism and antisemitism would be the obvious examples, while racism is perhaps too modern a phenomenon to count.

What is less obvious is that meat-eating is deep in the more important sense of being strongly, or inextricably, bound up with our well-being or with our willingness to embrace our humanity. It is this view of matters that Tanya Bernard's father may have been trying to articulate, and it is this view that often seems to form the background to familiar arguments for meat-eating, without being made explicit by means of the latter. The closest that many defenders of meat-eating come to clearly articulating the background picture is when they point out that we have canine teeth and this shows that in some sense we are naturally meat-eaters. If the background picture of what is natural and fulfilling is a realistic picture then vegetarians may have all sorts of clever and artful arguments but their practice goes against the grain of our being, or more simply, it goes against our human nature.

When someone makes the claim about dentition they are not entirely wrong although it is problematic to move from *what comes naturally to what we ought to do*. Some of the things that come naturally to us might not be so good. We have all sorts of laws and conventions that rein us in and are to everyone's advantage. But it is still tempting to say that a good diet must be, in some sense, a natural diet. Diets may be natural to creatures in ways that make them not just genetically fixed but also in ways that are related to the creatures' well-being. One familiar criticism of current approaches to intensive livestock farming is that they require an unnatural diet of grain to be forced upon herbivores (such as cows) as part of the race to get them to slaughter weight before the unfortunate creatures have time to fall ill. Going against their natural diet seems morally problematic. Similarly, even if the practice of recycling slaughterhouse waste back into the food chain by feeding it to dairy cows had not proven so devastatingly dangerous by resulting in BSE ('mad cow disease'), it might still be regarded as unnatural, and just plain wrong, to feed herbivores in this cannibalistic way. Similarly, although there are guidelines for feeding pets on vegetarian and vegan diets, even vegetarians or vegans might not consider it appropriate to do so because there is an obvious sense in which our pets are naturally carnivores and their carnivorous nature is bound up with our own history. We have tended to eat herbivores and to treat carnivores either as pets or else as dangerous rivals. Given this, it is no stretch of our intuitions to hold that, if we are to have pets, the most natural thing to do may also be the best thing to do. And this may involve feeding these companion animals with diets that relate closely to how their species have evolved.

Carried over into the human case, this line of thought may seem more troubling to vegetarians than it actually is. Our branch of the primate tree has resorted more frequently than others to carnivorous activity. We are closer to chimpanzees than to the stricter primate vegetarians or to occasional hunters, such as the relatively placid bonobos. And this divergence from the more vegetarian primates does seem to be of great antiquity. It is conceivable that meat-eating could have remained a deep requirement for human well-being. We might well have evolved into the kind of creatures who long for animal flesh in a way that would make its absence a deprivation. Without going too far into the rival accounts, one favoured view of Neanderthals (our nearest fully hominid relatives) is that they *were* reliant upon just the kind of diet that a picture of man the meat-eater conjures up. From what we know about them (which is much less than we would like to know), they seem to have pushed meat-eating to its farthest limits.

But our local branch of the human tree is more flexible. What our dentition suggests is not uniform meat-eating, but adaptability. This may have something to do with why we are still around and Neanderthals are not. Humans seem able to cope with a variety of mixed diets and to cope when meat is scarce or, for considerable stretches of time, virtually unavailable. Indeed, there is only one vitamin, B_{12} (cobalamin, usually present in commercial sources as cyanocobalamin) that we cannot source in adequate concentrations from a wild and completely non-animal diet. It can be sourced from fish, and this too may be a significant feature of our past given that fish is the only kind of meat that we may assume to have been continuously available to our ancestors without major interruptions. There are various hedged and conditional claims here, and if they are right they still do not make us naturally vegetarian or more ambiguously 'almost vegetarians'. Humans have always eaten meat when it has been available, and we have hunted animals not just for meat but for other vital resources such as skins, sinews, fat and bone. Some of us may still happen to have body metabolisms that fare better with a small meat component in our diet just as others may find meat too difficult to metabolize in comfort. At the margins, our bodies can behave in very different ways.

What the above does indicate is that our dietary flexibility makes most of us naturally able to cope with being vegetarians and vegan, with a little help from modern processing to source B_{12} (to produce insulation for nerve fibres and assist the reproduction of red blood cells) and, to be on the safe side, one or two other vitamins, such as vitamin D (to allow us to absorb calcium) during winter when there is less sunlight. Neither way of living is straightforwardly in tension with our evolved characteristics, but we may suspect that either would have been intolerable for Neanderthals if the suggested picture of them is even close to being accurate. In our own case, claims about medical health, or about our canine teeth, are at best a proxy for the background picture that represents meat-eating as integral to a fully natural or enriched way of being human. This same background picture might more effectively be brought into the foreground by claiming that a human life without the eating of meat must be missing something.

If this were true, vegetarianism would involve some significant loss or deficit. But it would seem trivial to suggest that the loss or deficit in question is simply the foregoing of various taste sensations, that what is missing from the vegetarian or the vegan life is the sheer sensory pleasure of meat, an exquisite or inimitable experience that vegetables, pulses, grains and tofu cannot provide. For someone whose life revolves around food, vegetarianism might well be understood as a restriction of this sort, as the ruling-out of possibilities, as self-imposed culinary exile. But this may seem a more appropriate attitude for a chef rather than the population at large. There are, after all, more important things than food when it is thought of in this manner. To tolerate harm to billions of animals (the figures may seem staggering but around 10 billion are killed for food in the United States alone) and to do so year after year, and to allow this to extend indefinitely into the future, without any prospect of an end, simply because we do not wish to abandon our favourite taste sensations, really does look like gluttony, or, if not gluttony, some manner of callous disregard.[10] Unless our other sources of sensory stimulation have become radically impoverished, this seems like a very poor reason to be a carnivore.

A slightly more significant human loss, but one that is only slightly more significant, could be loss of time. We do lead busy lifestyles and becoming vegetarian or vegan could eat into the time we need to get everything done. Becoming a vegetarian might be difficult, and becoming a vegan might be unimaginably time-consuming. But the kind of time-hungry lives that would make most sense of this charge, lives that so often involve more motion than direction, are a specifically modern phenomenon, and we might well think that such ways of living, rather than the taking of time over food preparation are the true loss to our humanity. (There is now a *Slow Food Movement* that champions just such a position, favouring an enjoyable pace for food preparation and for life in general.)[11] However, it is intelligible that other activities might be integral to human well-being and that time spend on food is time lost for these other matters. The busy parent with several children to look after may feel that there are just not enough hours in the day, although most of us are kept busy by matters that are less important than the demands of child rearing.

Michael Pollan, perhaps the best-known American champion of small ethical farming and an advocate of the value of eating ethically produced meat, articulates this concern about time troubles in his best-seller *The Omnivore's Dilemma*. He describes the impact of reading Peter Singer's case for vegetarianism (an appeal to minimize the sum total of suffering irrespective of the species of the victims) and his own subsequently (brief) experiment of living on a vegetarian diet. 'I find making a satisfying vegetarian dinner takes a lot more thought and work (chopping work in particular); eating meat is simply more convenient.'[12] I am not entirely sure that this problem would apply after the initial stage of learning to be either a vegetarian or a vegan. It may be a standard feature of any significant dietary change. Vegetables do, after all, cook more quickly than large hunks of meat. But at least for the stage that Pollan describes, he is probably right. During the process of becoming a vegetarian, *what am I going to eat?* can be a more or less daily question. You cannot just live out of the supermarket and grab the first thing that you see if you want to remain hale and hearty, or even in moderately good health. During the process of becoming a vegan, this same question of *what am I going to eat?* can be a several-times-a-day problem that often has no simple answer. Eating out is also more complicated, although some countries and some towns and cities have better reputations than others. Vegetarians, and more especially, vegans, may tend to become more aware of what they are putting into their bodies (which is a good thing) but the price of this knowledge can be a degree of inconvenience.

Even so, time troubles of this sort may seem relatively trivial when weighed against the harm of death to vast numbers of sentient creatures. Nobody likes to be inconvenienced, but there are limits to what most of us are prepared to do, or tolerate, in order to secure our own comfort. We would not personally slaughter animals in order to arrive home a little earlier. Suitably compassionate people, carnivores and vegetarians alike, may also go further and take the time to stop when they see an injured and clearly distressed animal by the roadside. If we need to free up time in order to do those things that make a life go well, we might, in any case, do so in any number of ways that have nothing to do with food. We might get up earlier in the day (in the way that humans have done for thousands of years) or come to terms with the fact that some of the material goals we pursue matter less than the time that we spend trying to get them. Alternatively, and less demandingly, we might watch less late-night television.

But Pollan does not build his case against vegetarianism only around the saving of time or around his own (quickly abandoned) dietary experiment. His case depends upon a broader attempt to picture vegetarianism and fast-food addiction as twin forms of modern alienation from what it is to be human. He is unusually direct in setting out what I have claimed is the standard background picture that shapes and motivates so many defences of meat-eating.

> Even if the vegetarian is a more highly evolved human being, it seems to me he has lost something along the way, something I'm not prepared to dismiss as trivial. Healthy and virtuous as I may feel these days I also feel alienated from traditions I value: cultural traditions like the Thanksgiving turkey, or even franks at the ballpark, and family traditions like my mother's beef brisket at Passover. These ritual meals link us to our history along multiple lines – family, religion, landscape, nation, and, if you want to go back much further, biology. For although humans no longer need meat in order to survive . . . we have been meat eaters for most of our time on earth.[13]

Some of what is said here connects to that rudimentary sense in which meat-eating is genuinely deep because of the way it is, historically, bound up with a wide range of human activities. And, of course, Pollan is nostalgic (so am I, it's not unusual). But beyond the nostalgia, he has made the important transition to direct claims about our humanity and about how we can lose sight of our connection not so much to nature *per se* but to our shared social world. This view of what it is to eat well and to live well as a human involves something more than a mistaken appeal to dubious conceptions of what is natural. It involves an appeal to history, community and tradition, to matters that have a real and direct claim upon us. To be fully human, to embrace what we are and to do so in the best manner available in the light of our history and culture, we are invited to accept our standing as both social beings and as 'carnivores', or, less disturbingly, as what Pollan calls 'omnivores', as beings who are open to all that is healthy and life-enriching, beings who are capable of accepting our place alongside others in a food-chain that not only involves but requires meat-eating.

Similar assumptions about meat-eating and about its centrality to human well-being can be found elsewhere, for example in Hugh Fearnley-Whittingstall's *River Cottage* books and in his succession of River Cottage programmes made for UK television. As a chef turned ethically informed smallholder, he has, at considerable personal inconvenience and even a degree of career risk, mounted a campaign to promote organic chicken at the expense of intensively reared chicken. And his books are laced with informed ethical commentary on why food matters. They are also marked by an infectious enthusiasm for wholesome food that is enjoyed as part of an experientially rich way of living. Peter Singer and Jim Mason comment that few people are more 'devoted to food' than Hugh Fearnley.[14] And this may be a fair assessment. Few people have done more to help shift popular perceptions of what is right and wrong about the way we treat livestock. Like Michael Pollan, he does not justify meat-eating by appeal to the (comparative) unimportance of animals or to any idea of a God who has put other animals here as our convenient walking larder. The shared view of Michael Pollan and of Hugh Fearnley is that without farming there would be no livestock and that it is better for the animal concerned that they live well, if briefly, and die at our hands rather than not having a chance to live at all.[15]

This involves an important argument, the *opportunity of life argument*, which I will focus upon in the next chapter, but whatever we might think of attempts to build a legitimating theory along these line, the shared picturing of how human contentment is compromised not by meat-eating but by industrialization and by industrialized food production is perhaps the most attractive alternative to vegetarianism and veganism. But while it is clear in Pollan and Hugh Fearnley that what motivates their rejection of vegetarianism is a background picture of meat-eating as integral to human well-being, it remains unclear just what the vegetarian or vegan would lose. Pollan writes about the vegetarian as someone who has 'lost something along the way', and specifies traditions and celebrations that involve meat-eating. But it is by no means clear that what matters in these cases is the meat rather than the celebration, or that the celebration requires the meat, or that the presence of vegetarians at the feast would in some way be a mood-dampening reproach to the carnivores. As noted above, Pollan prefers to use the term 'omnivores', but Hugh Fearnley is more forthright and is perhaps right to be so. We are far too fussy in our eating habits to qualify as true omnivores. Moreover, there are many things that even the most determined of meat-eaters accept as 'off limits' on grounds that involve disgust rather than culinary preference: Skunk Sundae, True Ratatouille and so on. (The reader may supply their own names for dishes that would remain unappealing even if they happened to taste good.)

What is relied upon by both Michael Pollan and Hugh Fearnley is not just a positive representation of the virtues and sociability of meat-eating, but a negative representation of vegetarianism as in some respects life-denying. This may seem unfair to vegetarians, but it is not so wholly inaccurate that it is an unrecognizable picture of things. Various historical instances of vegetarianism fit the picture quite well. We may think of the monastic vegetarianism of those who, in medieval times, restricted or abandoned their meat-eating as a deliberate attempt to mortify the flesh. Some Benedictine monks and Carmelite nuns still favour a vegetarian diet for related reasons that might not now be stated in such harsh terms. The hope of their medieval counterparts was one of figuratively killing off the body. What was human and transitory, rather than lasting and divine, was to be shunned and cast away. Such religious orders rejected the eating of meat because they bought into the picture that it was bound up with our humanity. But from their standpoint, humanity was disreputable. Their vegetarianism was as a form of renunciation, of both human desires and of a social world outside the monastery, a world in which meat-eating was bound up with pleasure and corporeal celebration.[16]

Other similar historic cases can be found. Monastic vegetarianism had its roots in the earlier vegetarianism of neo-Platonists like Porphyry (circa 232–305 C.E.), great thinkers who are sometimes quoted by contemporary vegetarians in an attempt to stress the antiquity and intellectual credentials of their way of living. But while the attitude of monastic and neo-Platonist vegetarians may strike us as, in significant respects, genuinely unattractive, it may also strike us as unrepresentative of what motivates and shapes contemporary vegetarianism. Even so, extreme cases can sometimes inform us about the less obvious aspects of a practice. They can make its faults stand out in relief.

Sources such as Pollan contribute to the idea that some of the historical problems remain in place, that vegetarianism is essentially renunciatory or has a slightly misanthropic and reproachful dimension to it. We may lack any specialized term for exactly what the core fault may be but 'puritanism' may capture some of its important aspects. This is also, up to a point, the version of vegetarianism that can still sometimes be found in more sympathetic sources, such as J. M.Coetzee's influential novel, *Elizabeth Costello*, a work of fiction that has stirred up a good deal of philosophical commentary since it was published in 1999. Its central character is an academic, the recipient of a prestigious literary award reaching the end of her life, who chooses to deliver two lectures on 'The Lives of Animals'. The lectures, also printed independently, form the core of the book. In them, the fictional Costello uses the opportunity to press her own sense of moral horror at our factory system, even to the point of drawing a familiar but controversial and unsettling parallel between the industrial processing of animals and the destruction of humans in the Holocaust. At a civilized meal afterwards, with fish tactfully served to the meat-eaters, the conversation remains strained. 'But your own vegetarianism,' says the President of the Faculty, 'it comes out of moral conviction, does it not?' Costello's reply is disturbing, 'No, I don't think so. . . . It comes out of a desire to save my soul.'[17] This is a woman who is not conventionally religious, but it is difficult not to hear the echoes of that earlier monastic and renunciatory vegetarianism still lingering in her words. She is, after all, a woman who sets herself apart from others, who can no longer fully participate in a shared world with the meat-eaters who surround her on all sides, people who are, for the most part, still in the midst of life while her own life is coming to an end.

Vegetarianism is sometimes treated in this way as a reproach, and it can genuinely be reproachful. A familiar stereotype here is of the vegetarian teenager who cannot bring herself to break-bread with a good will alongside carnivores, especially if they happen to be her parents. Meat-eaters, suspecting that this is the common judgmental situation, may be inclined to defence when they discover that their companion diner is a vegetarian or vegan. They may point out that these days, they hardly eat any meat, or that they could easily become a vegetarian if it wasn't for one or two minor pleasures that they would be reluctant to abandon. But being a vegetarian and even more so being vegan (because it is more demanding) can be such a personal matter that no reproach need ever be intended. Meat-eating is embedded in so much of our daily life, with most of us raised as meat-eaters, that personal reproach may be inappropriate in most ordinary contexts. There is also no reason why vegetarians or vegans should be incapable of seeing that it can be unwise to judge other people without much knowledge of why they live their lives in the way that they do. Most vegetarians have themselves, at some time, been meat-eaters, and some or many may also hold themselves to be an inappropriate authority to pass personal judgments about particular individuals as opposed to ethical judgments about the relative merits of various eating practices.

This presupposes that one need not take such a dim and misanthropic view of other humans that their dominant eating practice is placed on a par with complicity in the Holocaust. There are obvious dissimilarities as well as some technical points of comparison. Livestock are not slaughtered as vermin, as enemies or as social undesirables; nor need they be deliberately brutalized and demonized prior to their deaths; nor are they slaughtered by their own kind, in the grip of some combination of ideology and a sense of both unavoidable complicity and helplessness. Vegetarianism need not be tied to a problematic analogy with events so singular and dreadful that they have contributed in a unique way to our understanding of why we still need a concept of evil.

EATING WELL AND LIVING WELL

The apparently renunciatory aspect of vegetarianism is harder to deal with than the suggestion of reproach or misanthropy. After all, vegetarianism does involve foregoing something, and this may seem like a sacrifice of sorts. And where a practice has renunciation at its core, a charge of puritanism may also seem appropriate although a fuller discussion of puritanism will be postponed until Chapter 3.

What is difficult to reconcile with the idea of vegetarianism as essentially or above all renunciation is that vegetarians do not, typically, see their diet as a hardship. It is tempting to say that what is clearly given up is simply one set of taste sensations in favour of another. But it is intelligible that vegetarianism could involve renunciation of a more important sort. It could involve the sacrifice of an opportunity for a particular kind of good life. Michael Pollen and Hugh Fearnley take smallholding along traditional lines to be just such a good way of living, and it is easy to see why: it allows humans to be more connected to nature, to the seasonal cycle of rebirth and death and it allows those who live in this way an opportunity to recognize that we too are animals living in the midst of other creatures. These are claims that vegetarians and vegans need not dispute. I happen to be a vegan, but were I transported back to earlier times when farming and smallholding were the norm I would then have many good reasons to eat meat even if I could manage to avoid doing so. Were I to be a smallholder today, I would still have at least some of the same reasons for being a carnivore. But in neither case would these reasons involve the naturalness of meat-eating and the unnaturalness of vegetarianism. They would instead amount to a recognition that particular ways of being human can establish connections between meat-eating and well-being or (more realistically) living as well as one can given the constraints of circumstance.

I am not alone in this view. It is not idiosyncratic for vegetarians and vegans to regard their own dietary practice as a personal response to a current human situation, or to the question of *what kind of humans do we need to be or become if we are to have a viable future?* Vegetarianism and veganism can be regarded as a contributory response to a shared human predicament, rather than a way of being human that fits all people and every circumstance. Tanya Barnard articulates this same point well, albeit in terms that are normal for literature on food but rather less usual in discussions of philosophical ethics,

> There was a time when we were able to harvest vegetables from our gardens, eat our own chickens' eggs, drink our own cows' milk, and from these sources nourish our bodies. It was also possible to sustain ourselves by saving and using the seeds that our gardens offered. The sacred act of eating – to maintain our bodies' physical, mental, and spiritual well-being – should be so simple. Instead it has evolved into an exploitative act where factory farming, genetic engineering, and the increasing use of pesticides are now the norm.[18]

Setting aside the nostalgia, which vegans and vegetarians indulge in just as readily as carnivores, the over-riding point here is that meat-eating was (and presumably still is) bound up with living-well as a smallholder. But what most contemporary vegetarians and vegans abandon is only an isolated remnant of this way of living, an isolated practice now removed from the context that once made it important and, in an obvious way, more justifiable than it is now. There is nothing comparably deep or in touch with our humanity about eating at McDonald's, or eating out of Tesco and Wal-Mart. Shopping is not hunting; the collection of take-away food is not gathering or harvesting. Any of us can, if we have the resources, buy some land and try to re-establish the connection between living-well and the rearing and eating of animals. But this is not, for most of us, a realistic option. We do not have the money, the knowledge or the drive and psychological toughness required to learn the hard way. And without some such lifestyle, meat-eating is not deeply connected to our *well-being* unless we happen to be one of those individuals whose bodies fare better with a small meat component in their diet than they do with any vegetarian diet that they know or can readily access.

We are, for the most part, consumers of food and not its producers. And given a separation of most of us from any chance of supporting ourselves as producers, it is all too easy to understand just why so many of us have now begun to view food as a matter only of taste-sensations and fuel. This is not due solely to our lack of imagination. It is due in part to the way that the world has changed. All sorts of ties and connections that enabled us to regard food (and not just meat) in a different light have been severed, permanently.

Given this, it may also be easier to understand just why vegetarians tend not to see their own diet as a hardship. Nothing important and accessible is lost. The eating of animals is not usually regarded in the medieval manner as a desirable activity that is stoically declined. Rather, ceasing to be vegetarian is something that is understandably regard as a loss, although again, it may be difficult to pin down the loss in question, but loss of identity might figure somewhere. In this respect, eating vegetarian can be thought of as analogous, in some respects, to eating kosher (i.e. to respecting the law of kashruth). To eat kosher also involves an element of renunciation. It is a carnivorous diet in which some creatures, pigs for example, are off the menu. More generally, large land animals that do not graze and have cloven hoofs are not to be eaten.[19] But it would be odd to regard contemporary kosher cuisine as a form of culinary hardship. And this may not be simply because one set of animals is available as a substitute for other prohibited creatures. The point is, rather, that kosher food is rich, varied and celebratory. There is an element of ruling-out, but there is no farewell to pleasure. Restriction as a part of dietary practice may involve something other than sacrifice. It may be a way in which identities are defined and maintained.

More simply, if we have a richer conception of food than one that treats it only as fuel or as a source of taste sensations, then, through our eating practices we may express our sense of who we are, of what we value and of how we aspire to live. Eating kosher serves as an example because it is, above all, about belonging to a tradition; ethical vegetarianism, by contrast, is about an appreciation of the value of other creatures. Both have something positive at their core, and in this respect both make an implicit connection between the idea of eating-well and the idea of well-being or, more broadly of living-well. The latter has always required that some things must remain off limits.

From an ethical point of view, food matters because it is one of the ways in which our relations to each other, to other creatures and to the environment in general, are established. For those who find this conception of eating-well a little too vague, I will suggest that it involves things of the following sort: enjoyment in and through food; nutritional appropriateness given the condition that we are in; a degree of honesty about what we are eating; some rudimentary knowledge about how our food was produced; eating in a way that enriches our relations with other humans (e.g. it should not involve habitual solitary consumption); eating in a way that is consistent with our values and/or expresses those values; having values that are themselves of a reasonable and defensible sort; eating in a way that involves a practical aware-ness of the importance of other humans, other creatures and our shared environment.

This conception of *eating-well* does not automatically require us to be carnivores or to be vegetarians, but it does entail that eating enriches our lives when it is a richly expressive practice and when the values it expresses are defensible and, more par-ticularly, appropriate for the best kinds of lives that are available to us. Viewed in this light, vegetarianism can be seen as an attract-ive and positive option because of its expressive component and because of the worthwhile values that it happens to express. But, as with the advocacy of meat-eating by Tanya Bernard's father, claims about its contribution to well-being may often masquer-ade as claims about nutrition or health. It is, for example, often asserted that vegetarianism can significantly reduce the risk of heart disease, stroke, obesity, type-2 diabetes and perhaps even some forms of cancer. And it does seem to be a good diet for children.[20] These are significant health considerations, but such claims can also serve as a proxy for the ethically more important claim that vegetarianism is beneficial in a way that can be bound up with well-being in a more than medical sense, a sense that concerns the living of a good life. But to indicate the contribution that vegetarianism can make to our well-being does not establish any unique connection that it has to the latter. Ethically informed varieties of meat-eating may turn out to fare just as well. Even so, recognizing the connection to our well-being may be enough to prevent vegetarianism from being disadvantaged at the outset of our enquiry and disadvantaged in a way that no argument about its merits would be liable to remove.

2 An Unwritten Contract?

RECIPROCATION

I have suggested that ethical vegetarianism can contribute to eating-well and to living-well, but it is not the only dietary option that offers such advantages. Other ways of living, other ways of being human, can express important values and in particular they can show and even embody our practical commitment to the importance of other creatures and perhaps also of the environment that we share with them. Of these, other ways of living the most obvious are what we might call ethically informed smallholding and hunter-gathering, although the closest that most of us could come to the former is through buying ethically, and the latter is no longer an option of any sort in the United Kingdom or United States. (It is scarcely an option anywhere else.) Hunter-gathering is, however, a paradigm of valuing other creatures while remaining a carnivore. Consider the following advice of a Sioux elder to his son,

> shoot your four-legged brother in the hind area, slowing it down but not killing it. Then take the four-legged's head in your hands, and look into his eyes. The eyes are where all the suffering is. Look into your brother's eyes and feel his pain. Then take your knife and cut the four-legged under his chin, here on the neck, so that he dies quickly. And as you do, ask your brother, the four-legged, for forgiveness for

what you do. Offer also a prayer of thanks to your four-legged kin for offering his body to you just now, when you need food to eat and clothing to wear. And promise the four-legged that you will put yourself back into the earth when you die, to become the nourishment of the earth, and for the sister flowers, and for the brother deer. It is appropriate that you should offer this blessing for the four-legged and, in due time reciprocate.[1]

This may be a somewhat idealized picture of how one particular group of Native Americans once survived. Even if accurate it may also have emerged in part as a practical response to an earlier phase of over-hunting. Be that as it may there is an important requirement of mutuality or reciprocity built into the above picture of what it is to take an animal's life. The hunter imaginatively tries to think himself into the animal's situation, not just in a way that makes him a more efficient hunter but in a way that leads him to accept the need for reparation or atonement. Here, we may feel inclined to say *so what, the animal still ends up dead*, but at least its life will have been lived out under conditions to which the hunter and those who have gone before him may have contributed in a positive way. And there have been times in human history when this is the best that we could manage. From the standpoint of the *well-being* of the animals, we may also suspect that they would be better off under a system of hunting and gathering rather than under the present system of intensive farming and industrial slaughter.

The idea of reciprocity has, historically, taken a more specialized form in justifications of farming. That we corral animals, order and structure their lives, breed them selectively and so on suggests that we see them not as fellow creatures but as much less important than us. If we are of a mind to quote Genesis we might claim to have something akin to a legitimate 'dominion' over them. But this belief in our superiority has often been tempered by the idea that our entitlements come with significant strings attached. Relying upon metaphor and figurative language,

we may speak of our stewardship of wild creatures, or more prob-
lematically of a covenant (usually an 'ancient covenant') or contract with creatures whose ancestors were wild but who have
long since fallen under our sway. In a recent collection of essays
on *The Future of Animal Farming*, Bernard Rollin writes in this
way of 'the modern human abrogation of our ancient contract
with animals and with the earth, which contract nourished and
sustained the growth of our civilization'.[2]

It is easy for ethically driven vegetarians and vegans to sym-
pathize with this way of thinking as a far better option than the
norm. (Peter Singer supplies the introduction to the above volume for just this reason.) Some may even accept the legitimacy
of these claims and treat ethical farming as a defensible way of
living. But the very idea of a contract is a problematic way of
understanding how creatures of any sort relate to one another. It
is problematic when presented as an account of human relations
and human institutions (via the idea that we are participants in a
'social contract'), and it is even more problematic as a justification
of meat-eating and of breeding animals for slaughter. A tension
here arises in the latter case because slaughter involves harm of
an extreme sort, and what kind of creature would agree to that?
Another issue is the absence of a shared language in which the
terms of any deal could be negotiated. To some contemporary
advocates of a 'social contract' theory, notably John Rawls, this
impracticality of an actual agreement has seemed to rule out
the idea that human/animal relations can be understood in
contractual terms.[3]

But here we need not push the metaphor of a contract too
far or expect to find anything that could closely resemble an
actual or explicit agreement in order to recognize that a specialized and interesting form of reciprocity is being claimed. In the
above life picture of the Sioux elder, the life of a fellow creature
ought not to be taken without giving something in return, even
if it is something that cannot be of quite the same value. As
a result, the reciprocation in question does not look at all like a

commercial transaction. The hunter gives what they can but this may not be enough to make the arrangement one of mutual advantage rather than necessity. By contrast the idea of an ancient covenant or, more prosaically, of a human/animal contract is invoked to suggest something more akin to humans and animals being combined together in a situation of mutual advantage. And this, in some respects, is more akin to an idealized commercial arrangement: each side gains.

Odd though we may find this, when part of the deal on offer involves being killed, it is an idea that has a long history. In her classic treatment of kashruth dietary prohibitions, Mary Douglas points out that the idea of abomination may be read in multiple ways. It may be read in a way that makes certain kinds of animals a source of disgust, or in a way that makes that taking of their lives for food a dreadful act because they are outside of a special and mutually beneficial relationship with us,

> Of land animals, the people of Israel may only eat those which are also allowed to be sacrificed on the altar, which restricts them to eating only the species of land animals which depend on the herdsmen entirely for safety and sustenance.[4]

The Roman poet Lucretius, writing in the first-century BCE, writes in a similar vein but without paralleling the relation of humans to animals with that between humans and a God or gods. Although he writes movingly of the suffering of cattle when their calves are killed, Lucretius points out that they are nonetheless given protection and shelter in return for 'their services' and this seems justification enough to require the latter.[5]

Whatever the precedents, the idea of mutual advantage may still seem strained, but it would be ungenerous to fail to recognize at least that the day-to-day experience of those who work with livestock often is one of care, even in those early hours of winter mornings when vegetarians and vegans like myself are still ensconced in bed. To think of this simply as looking after the product rather than looking after the animals' interests might be to miss what it is about the farming of livestock that makes it so difficult to give up even when it leads, as it so often does, to personal hardship and a mountain of debt.

Moreover, the benefits that animals can derive from the farm environment can be all too real and tangible. Outside of the farm, there is a world where hunger and predation are common. It is a world where many of our farmed animals would probably not survive for very long (pigs probably would, maybe some cows, depending upon the location, and one or two other animals also). True, this is a dependence for which generations of humans are responsible. We, or at least our ancestors and predecessors, have selectively bred for infantile characteristics. But even so, inside the farm, there is the offer of care and shelter, at least for a time. If nature really is quite so 'blood red in tooth and claw' as Darwin once suggested, the security of the farmyard could be worth having in spite of the obvious downside. The arrangement could, overall, be one of mutual advantage.

THE INTERESTS OF FARMED ANIMALS

It may help to clarify the idea of an unwritten contract if we trim away some of the excessive and vulnerable claims that have become associated with it. The first of these is that the deal is in some way rooted in a historic 'choice' that was made by the wild ancestors of today's domesticated animals. The use of 'choice' here is just as figurative as the idea of a contract itself. There is no suggestion that animals have ever had an overall grasp of the nature of the arrangement in question. The best-known account of such a historic, but figurative, choice is *The Covenant of the Wild* (1992) by Stephen Budiansky, a popular US author on scientific matters and a smallholder in Maryland.

According to Budiansky, 'in an evolutionary sense, domesticated animals chose us as much as we chose them.'[6] The domestication of livestock did not result from capture and deferred slaughter (the way things are usually assumed to have occurred). Instead, wild animals attached themselves to human communities in return for scavenging opportunities and protection from predation. They stayed on in spite of the periodic practice of slaughter. This *staying on* was, figuratively, the choice that they made. And from an evolutionary point of view they were right to do so. Domesticated species have proliferated, while other species have declined. In the light of this historical alignment of their species interests with ours, when we try to make sense of the position of today's domesticated animals we should not be asking 'what's in it for us' but 'what's in it for them.'[7] Michael Pollan embraces Budiansky's narrative wholeheartedly; Hugh Fearnley-Whittingstall finds it persuasive but retains a degree of caution.

At best this is conjectural narrative and some parts of it sound more plausible than others. It may work as an explanation of the domestication of dogs, and indeed this is Budiansky's model for all domestication, but to elide over the differences between the domestication of dogs and the domestication of livestock is problematic. An appeal to scavenging from campfires and middens does no real work in the case of herbivores such as cows and sheep, and an appeal to protection from predators seems questionable. Herd animals have always had their own perfectly good, tried and tested survival strategy: be part of a large group, don't stand out from the crowd and keep on the move when there are too many predators around or if the group starts to look small. There are, of course, some livestock animals, such as pigs, who will eat more or less anything and the scavenging story works better in the case of their wild boar ancestors. But wild boar are elusive, and by repute mysterious creatures, natural woodland dwellers who keep themselves apart from humans. Even their domesticated pig descendents still have to be socialized into tolerating a human presence. They can still hold up the operation of a slaughterhouse if they see that there are humans ahead. The prospect of wild boar rolling into camp, abandoning the woods and staying around after seeing one of their number slaughtered (and presumably drained) may seem remote.

While we may appreciate the attractions of Budiansky's narrative to the champions of ethically informed livestock rearing and to defenders of the idea of an unwritten contract, the contract idea does not need to depend upon historical claims of this sort. A standard move in discussions of the idea that human institutions and practices are similarly legitimated by an unwritten 'social contract' is to treat the contract not as a historic event but as a hypothetical agreement, one that we would enter into if matters were made clear to us and we were given a choice. There has, in the past, been a temptation for some philosophers to make sense of the 'social contract' idea in more or less literal and historic terms, but this may be not just false but unhelpful and unnecessary. Why, after all, would *we* still be bound to accept a contract entered into by our ancestors, unless it was reasonable for us to do so on independent grounds and by appeal to our own situation? And here it may seem that these independent grounds are what really matters.

The idea of a hypothetical contract is preferable in the case of animals not just because of the vulnerability of any historical conjecture, but because historical conjectures do not give suitable content to the idea of even a figurative agreement between animals and humans. In Budiansky's account, for example, the animals are supposed to have stayed around, but without any grasp of the arrangement that would result. To speak of this as a figurative choice by the first livestock may be a misleading way to put matters. By contrast, a hypothetical contract can make much more sense of the idea of entering into a mutually advantageous arrangement. And here it is probably better not to appeal to a magical scenario in which we can converse with animals, but rather we may appeal to a situation in which the interests of animals are spoken for by some suitably well-informed human interlocutor, someone whose *only* interests are in animal well-being. Other more complicated scenarios may be constructed, and just so long as they are hypothetical scenarios they will do their work in much the same way.

Elizabeth Telfer, although hostile to the idea of an unwritten contract, nevertheless gives a good summary of what its terms might be.

> In this hypothetical bargain, the animals live more comfortably than in the wild – food and shelter are easier to find, they are protected from diseases and parasites and they die humanely; but they die sooner than they would otherwise, and the occasion of their death is planned and controlled in a way that it would not be if they died naturally or fell to a predator. The bargain is hypothetical because although no individual makes a choice, the price paid for the benefits can still be said to be a reasonable one.[8]

The problem involved in getting the hypothetical contract off the ground is not that there is an absence of care in farming, or at least farming of the best sort, but that that even under the most ethically informed conditions, the bargain still seems like a very poor one. There may be an element of protection given to domesticated livestock, but protection that is to some extent necessitated by the prior actions of humans. Animals in the wild are always vulnerable, but we are the ones who have bred certain of our farm animals to be incapable of defending themselves. Moreover, the protection that we then offer is inseparable from harm at a very young age, as little as 6 weeks in the case of chickens, that is only 42 days of life for the single largest group of livestock that we currently rear. Matters are slightly better for cows and sheep. They live past a year, but still die while they are very young. Even if we were to imagine some heavily enriched animal lifestyle where every good thing was supplied, it might still be difficult to see it as worth the terrible price that is exacted.

Telfer points to Richard Adams' *Watership Down* to reinforce the point. In this well-known story, a group of rabbits, on the run, and in search of a new home, come across a warren where everyone seems to live well and without hunger or day-to-day fear. The life on offer is even, in some respects, culturally rich and includes various goods and pleasures more readily associated a well-lived human life than with a life that would make any sense for a rabbit. No matter, these goods serve as a stand-in for whatever kind of enrichment an animal life could actually benefit from. In return for this plenty and safety, there is periodic slaughter by the farmer. When the book's central characters find this out, they set off again on their journey to a truer home. The judgement of those with their best interests at heart is that the deal on offer is not worth having. But what helps to make sense of this fictional preference (couched as it is in anthropomorphic terms) is that the rabbits happen to have some other viable option. They can go elsewhere to live. The farmer is, in this respect, an interloper and not a neces-sary, built-in feature of their lives. But what this scenario does not capture is that the opportunity of life may itself depend upon the deal. The farming system and/or the farmer's own inter-vention may be required for an animal to come into existence in the first place. And this places us in a much more grey area.

Were we all vegetarians, there would still be wild creatures (perhaps more of them) and perhaps some of the animals cur-rently reared as livestock would also still be around, albeit living very different lives. But most of our current livestock would never have been bred. They were bred only and specifically because we have a practice of meat-eating. Most of our livestock would not be here otherwise. In the light of this, the deal on offer may have a significant downside (premature death by slaughter), but it may now seem to be a much better deal because, as Hugh Fearnley remarks 'short, domesticated lives are, on balance, better than no life at all.'[9]

THE OPPORTUNITY OF LIFE ARGUMENT

The position set out above may be labelled the *opportunity of life argument*. What it aims to show is that livestock rearing and meat-eating are in the interest of livestock. This might not be an over-riding consideration. We may have various side-constraints upon what is morally tolerable and intolerable, but if the argument is sound it will highlight an important and *potentially* decisive consideration. The argument directs our attention towards the interests of the animals themselves rather than our own moral sensibilities (important though these are). This may, at the very least, allow us to dispose of a familiar knock-down objection. Suppose we allow that the efforts of a farmer or smallholder have resulted in an animal being alive, and let us also suppose that we set aside all the other contributory factors. This will still not justify their taking the animal's life or causing it to be taken, because we have no automatic and general right to destroy our own creations. It would not, for example, have been right for Leonardo to destroy the Mona Lisa even though he was the one who painted it. The creator or owners of something may have a preference, but this need not, on its own, be a good enough justification for its destruction or, in the case of a creature, its killing.

Considerations apart from the owners' preference are significant, but in the two cases these turn out to be considerations of different sorts. In the case of the painting, it has no interest in the way that an animal has an interest. What matters instead is its relation to other humans. Over time, artworks can come to have a cultural significance to successive generation. This would probably lead us to oppose destruction even by the artist if they could be magicked through time and were still able to demonstrate a legal entitlement to it. But the artist might, more plausibly, have an entitlement to destroy the painting prior to its having acquired this cultural significance. In the case of the animal, what matters above all is the animal's own interest. If it could be shown that, in spite of appearances to the contrary, some animal has an overall interest in being part of a system that ultimately requires its slaughter, then this consideration could weight our deliberation towards allowing the 'destruction' to take place. The killing would then be justifiable by appeal to animal interests and not the curious desires or whims of its purported owner or 'creator'.

Showing that some or other animal or animals do have such an interest in the system that ultimately kills them will depend upon getting the *opportunity of life argument* to work, and that may seem like a tall order. This is partly because it is initially counter-intuitive, but partly because it is usually formulated in ways that are immediately suspect. In philosophical circles, the best-known formulation of the argument is drawn from Leslie Stephen's polemic against vegetarianism in *Social Rights and Duties* (1896), 'Of all the arguments for Vegetarianism none is so weak as the argument from humanity. The pig has a stronger interest than anyone in the demand for bacon. If all the world were Jewish, there would be no pigs at all.'[10] The tone here is one of bluff, no-nonsense, commonsense, but the choice of animal may intro-duce unwelcome complications. Some pigs could readily be returned to the wild and *that* would better serve their interest. Relatedly, they are disturbingly intelligent creatures (the usual comparison is with a fairly smart dog), and this gives some meat-eaters qualms about eating pigs. Stephens' side-swipe at Judaism also clouds the issue. A more straightforward appeal to a trade-off between slaughter and existence may eliminate these unhelpful distractions.[11]

In response to this, unlike the case of exchanging care for slaughter, there is no point in appealing to the shortness of the life on offer. No matter how brief a life turns out to be, as long as it is a life that is worth living it will be worth the loss that comes at the (premature) end. As Hugh Fearnley points out, 'Premature slaughter is not the best part of the deal but it is, nonetheless, part of the deal.'[12]

Nevertheless, even in this formulation, the argument is under-constrained. The opportunity of a life is no good at all if the life on offer is not worth living. In the case of industrialized farming, it can be far from obvious that the only life available is better than non-existence. Sometimes it will be, but often it will not.

Many different systems of farming (including what is sometimes called 'big organic') are industrialized, and some can offer the animals more life-opportunities than others. But industrialized systems tend to have precisely the faults that animal activists and ethically informed farmers point out: mortality rates are high and indicative of routine suffering; animals are bred to put on meat rather than bred for health, and the inclusion of antibiotics in their feed is a standard way to get them up to slaughter-weight before they deteriorate as a result of intensive feeds and inbred-vulnerabilities. Even dairy farming can have a dreadful aspect. The removal of calves from mothers can be extremely traumatic. The mothers can bellow for days afterwards and may show symptoms not unlike a rudimentary form of bereavement.[13] Given the level of suffering that is standardly inflicted upon livestock by the more intensive systems, in many cases, though not all, it might well be better if the animals in question had never lived rather than going through what is required of them.

By contrast, a life lived out on pasture and with good conditions of care, and with good chances to express a wide range of natural behaviours, amounts to a life that is (in most cases at least) clearly worth living, no matter how short it then turns out to be. To try to get the *opportunity of life argument* to justify anything other than the later may involve demanding too much. With this qualification in mind what we now have is an *opportunity of life argument* that is pared back to the following: to enjoy life at all, some animals have to be born into the world as livestock, otherwise they simply would not be born. Where the animals born into this system enjoy lives that are worth living, as they are in the case of ethically informed farming, they benefit from the practices of meat-eating and of livestock rearing. Consequently, someone whose dominant concern was the animals' own best interests would on behalf of the animals themselves support these practices.

One problematic feature of the *opportunity of life argument*, even when stated in this qualified manner, is that if it proves anything at all it seems to prove too much. It would, after all, seem to legitimate the slaughter of animals irrespective of their characteristics and traits. It would legitimate or at least give us an important reason to support or tolerate the slaughter of animals that we would be deeply reluctant to kill, such as primates or even humans. If primates were farmed commercially for their meat, there would no doubt be a great many more of them around. Their interests in existing might be served by such a system. But we recoil at the prospect. And we would recoil even more at any scenario in which humans were bred and reared for slaughter. We would then be in a situation not unlike the option suggested by Jonathan Swift's satirical *Modest Proposal* (1729) suggesting that the combined problems of poverty and overpopulation in Ireland could be solved by the selling of infants to the English for meat.

Part of what makes Swift's scenario humorous rather than simply appalling is that someone who genuinely campaigned for this policy would not strike us as mistaken or morally different, but as mentally disturbed. It is not an option that is, or could be, on the table. Special considerations are normally taken to apply in the case of humans, considerations that would make their routine killing for food unthinkable under anything short of fictionally extreme circumstances. The considerations in question might involve their human rights, but we may be inclined to the view that eating children would not just be a violation of their rights but would in some deeper way, be morally horrific and not just wrong. Talk of 'rights' here may serve only as a proxy for the difficult idea of wrongdoing beyond the ordinary bounds of vice and beyond reasonable consideration. Operating a system of human slaughter would be much worse than not bringing the humans in question into existence even if it was in their interests to live a short and functional life.

We may also be inclined to hold that a comparable system of animal slaughter is not horrific in the same way, and this may seem to place us in danger of lapsing into some form of pro-human prejudice that claims a special privileged standing for humans and thereby risks loosing sight of the fact that we too are animals. The now-familiar name for such prejudice is 'speciesism'. One way around this problem would be to bluntly assert that we do matter a great deal more than any other sort of creature. But we need not adopt this defence. An appeal to the moral horror of systematically breeding humans for slaughter can be based upon the dreadfulness of cannibalism, or more restrictively, the practice of cannibalism by any reasonably intelligent social animal. After all, we strongly disapprove of cannibalistic chimps, and their own companions seem to share this disapproval. If any social animal is to live well, in line with its biological traits, then some threats from its companions must, after all, be removed and one obvious way to do this is to have a clear distinction between companions, or even potential-companions, and food. Cannibalism still happens but it is exceptional and deeply taboo. Our intuitions about this matter, at least in the case of humans and primates, extend to livestock. Many of us do not mind eating beef, but the BSE scare revealed unease about feeding parts of cows to other cows, chickens to other chickens and so on.

There is something that we usually accept to be wrong about cannibalism that many of us do not hold to be wrong about meat-eating per se. And here, cannibalism may be thought of in broad terms, humans feeding other humans to dogs as pet food would be just as repellent, it would be cannibalism by proxy. And humans eating primates may seem too close for comfort. We may note that some forest tribes eat spider monkeys (under resource pressures or as an offshoot of a reprehensible trade in bush-meat) and we may be aware of colobus monkeys being hunted and eaten by chimpanzees, but these too fill us with unease. Faced with the prospect of a 'beneficial' system of breeding humans for food, the defender of *the opportunity of life argument* can point out that our refusal to countenance any such system need not be regarded as a form of speciesism, it involves moral considerations of a different and species-neutral sort.

WHICH ANIMALS BENEFIT AND WHEN?

More significant difficulties for the *opportunity of life argument* emerge when it is required to be precise without becoming counter-intuitive. It is, in the version considered so far, clear enough about *what* livestock animals are supposed to benefit from and *what* they have an interest in. The point of the argument is to show that they have an interest in the overall system of meat-rearing, a system or package-deal that combines the practices of slaughter and of meat-eating together with breeding and rearing. But it is less clear about exactly *which* animals have this interest and *when* they have it. If I were to suggest that some currently existing animal about to have its throat cut still, even at this late moment, has an interest in the continuation of meat-rearing, this might well seem like an odd suggestion.

So I repeat the question: *which* animals have an interest in meat-rearing and *when* do they have this interest? When someone points out that animals facing slaughter would not exist without the system of slaughter they may be stating a truth, but it is equally true that the animals in question are *already* alive and do not *now* need the meat-rearing system to bring them into existence. Were the system to end, they could still be around and might live ten times longer. And it is considerations of this sort that make the ending of the system appear to be *now* in their best interests.

It might still be argued that meat-rearing is fair, but not by virtue of serving the current interests of livestock when they are about to face the blade, but by virtue of serving some interest that they had at a prior time. Our temptation here may be to say that the system serves their interests while they are alive but prior to slaughter. However, as long as they are alive the only advantages that the system can offer will be a matter of care and protection necessitated by the prior actions of humans. And, we have already seen that exchanging slaughter for this would be a dubious trade-off.

What this may lead to is the awkward realization that the *opportunity of life argument* is not a robust expression of bluff common sense. It is, in what may be its most defensible version, a metaphysical argument of a difficult sort. Already living creatures do not need to be brought into existence and have no current interest in a trade-off between existence and slaughter. They are already, palpably *there*. The argument will only work by appeal to the interests of animals *prior* to their existence. Animals that do not yet exist may have an interest that the meat-rearing system serves. Without the latter, they may never come into existence.

And this is precisely what is sometimes taken to give the argument force when it is used not as a positive case for meat-rearing, but as a negative assault upon vegetarianism: the latter threatens to block the passage into existence for vast numbers of animals. The animals in question are not the animals in our fields, dry-lots or barns. They are the animals that are yet-to-be and may, as such, seem more akin to fictions than to real, tangible, flesh-and-blood creatures. Once it is realized that the argument is about the interests of creatures that do not yet exist, a bluff no-nonsense response may seem in order. And this is exactly what the traditional vegetarian response supplies. A classic early twentieth-century vegetarian text, Henry Salt's 'The Logic of the Larder', puts matters bluntly,

> A person who is already in existence may feel that he would rather have lived than not, but he must first have the *terra firma* of existence to argue from; the moment he begins to argue from the abyss of the non-existent, he talks nonsense.[14]

When carried over into the case of other animals Salt's point is clear, once animals exist they do not need meat-rearing to bring them into existence, but prior to their existence they have no interests at all.

But this cannot be quite right. This response may make it difficult to make any sense of our having obligations to future generations, none who whose members currently enjoy existence. It may also erode our ability to appreciate ourselves as human beings who occupy only a tiny segment of a much larger unfolding reality and who can intelligibly care about the greater part of it that lies beyond our own tiny segment.

In more prosaic terms, Salt obscures an important distinction between animals that do not yet exist and animals that will never exist. The latter really do not have any interests at all. We might speak about their interests only in certain kinds of fiction such as thought experiments. But it is not nonsense to speak about the interests of animals that will exist, but do not yet happen to do so. In their case, it may also be intelligible to speak about interests that they can have prior to their existence. Interests do not presuppose that creatures have already attained what Salt referred to as the *terra firma* of existence. This may initially seem a little abstract, but the point can be made clearer if we consider a couple of examples.

The first example is from Peter Singer, a one-time supporter of Salt's response, who has long since come to view the *opportunity of life argument* as too powerful to be answered so easily,

> After all, most of us would agree that it would be wrong to bring a child into the world if we knew, before the child was conceived, that it would have a genetic defect that would make its life brief and miserable. To conceive such a child is to cause it harm.[15]

It is important to note here that the harmed child is one that actually comes into existence but its interests seem to date from before its life.

The second example is from Bernard Rollin's work on the ethics of genetically engineered livestock. Rollin advances what he calls the 'conservation of welfare' principle: *no genetic engineering should be permitted if it results in an animal that is worse off than a non-genetically engineered animal in comparable circumstances.*[16] Whether or not we accept Rollin's principle (commercial food manufacturers are unlikely to do so) it again gives us purchase upon the idea that for an animal to be brought into existence in a particular manner may involve a form of harm. Such animals seem to have an interest that predates their existence, an interest that concerns what is done in order to bring them into being.

In both cases, interests do not presuppose the *terra firma* of existence, but they do presuppose that the creature in question comes to exist at some point in time. What this leans in the direction of is a position that contemporary philosophers call the Prior Existence View, the view that creatures already have interests if they already exist or if is it the case that they are going to exist.[17] This amounts to an acceptance that Salt's response is mistaken. But it is a rather involved philosophical position and does not give the advocate of the *opportunity of life argument* quite what they may have been looking for. On this view, vegetarianism turns out not to cause any harm by blocking off existence because only creatures that do eventually come into existence can be harmed. However, those creatures that do come into a worthwhile existence as livestock may perhaps be said to have a genuine interest in the continuation of the meat-rearing system if they would not come into a worthwhile existence without the latter.

What complicates matters is that they seem to have this interest prior to existence but not during it. They do not obviously have an interest in the meat-rearing system once they are alive and they certainly do not have it at the time of slaughter. Once alive, their interests may well lie just where vegetarians have always suggested, in an end to meat-rearing. And this leaves us with the difficult question of which interests should take precedence.

The *opportunity of life argument*, once set out in a way that is sensitive to the above points, will direct our attention towards the interests that current livestock previously had, and the interests that other animals, ones that are going to exist in the future, already but temporarily have. And this may give some sense to talk of mutual interests and more figuratively of an unwritten contract. Vegetarians, on the other hand, may favour the current interests of actually existing creatures. While it may be tempting to say that the latter are obviously more important, it may be difficult to do so without endorsing short-term pre-occupations or an unwillingness to place currently existing creatures, including ourselves, in a much larger context.

What we have reached is an argumentative stalemate of a familiar sort, a situation in which rival considerations can be balanced up against each other but no single consideration obviously trumps the others. On the one hand, the *opportunity of life argument* does real work, less work than its supporters hope, although still enough to give some justification for continuing with ethically informed meat-rearing. It is the means by which animals come into existence and enjoy some approximation to a good, if short life. As such, it may only serve a restricted cluster of animal interests, but it can be seen as, up to a point, mutually advantageous. Ethical vegetarianism, on the other hand, might better serve the interests of already existing creatures. Those who are vegetarians because of the latter are vegetarians for a good reason.

3 Vegetarianism and Puritanism

FOOD WITHOUT HISTORY

While we might not think that *meat is murder* (a slogan from the 1970s that few vegetarians now seem happy to adopt), it does nonetheless originate in an act of violence, of deliberately inflicted physical trauma of a sort that we would not use to end the life of a pet or the life of a fellow human even if they were in extreme pain. Violence of this sort does not just end a life, it strips away a sense of creaturely dignity and helps turn animals into something more easily regarded as raw material. So, let us simply take it that slaughterhouses are not pleasant places. They are, for most of us, akin to non-places, locations where the normal rules seem to be suspended, places that we do not go. We might be happy to feed animals to our offspring, but we would be reluctant to take infants for an educational tour through the local abattoir. We might, vegetarians and meat-eaters alike, have enough difficulty steadying our own nerves for such an undertaking.

Some defenders of meat-eating might be perfectly happy to accept this as a reasonable unease about the ending of animal lives. Others might regard it as sentimentality. But such criticism may fail to acknowledge the way in which emotions can track the world and can, in some cases, count as an awareness of its more disturbing features. To be unsettled by the death of animals is not obviously a weakness on the part of squeamish consumers.

When fears of foot-and-mouth disease were at their height in Britain during the 2001 outbreak and television carried pictures of the piles of animal carcases, it was a pitiful sight, one that reduced farmers to tears. Partly their response may be associated with the loss of years of work to build up particular blood-lines and herds. But it would seem odd to suggest that it had nothing to do with the harm suffered by creatures they had cared for, creatures killed *en masse* and before their time. Yet these were, in many cases, animals who would have been packed off to the slaughterhouse within a few months of their earlier demise. The distress of farmers could be regarded as symptomatic of the increasing distance between farming and slaughter, a separation between the farm as a caring environment and the abattoir as a more specialized location where care and harm are mixed, but where only the latter is indispensable. Only in a slaughterhouse would distress at death be utterly debilitating.

It has often been said that if our slaughterhouses had glass walls, there would be few meat-eaters left. It is a claim that may be worth repeating, but it is not necessarily true. We can, after all, become accustomed to many things. Those who work in slaughterhouses may or may not like their work but they do not seem to find the job unbearable. Their predicament is, perhaps, akin to that of medical students who do not quit at the first sight of a body but instead adopt an attitude of 'interest' and sometimes of bravado, aiming to show, conspicuously, that they are not overawed by the presence of death and the awareness it can bring of one's own mortality. The rest of us do not have to encounter the killing of animals head-on. We can, instead, look the other way. But this too is a way of being aware. It involves recognition that there may be something dreadful to look away from. And what we try not to notice, or to dwell upon, is a process that is in many cases, nearby. Most of us are unlikely to be more than half an hour's drive from a slaughterhouse. As I write, I am approximately 1000 metres away from a site of animal slaughter, a hidden single-storey building with its own special approach road and secure gate. Without the occasional and well-publicized escapes by animals, I might never have realized that it was there. But it is. And it has counterparts elsewhere although, given their sequestered and isolated nature, it would be easy for someone to pretend that the meat on their plate has not come from such a place, that it does not originate in an act of violent harm, and that it is food without any unsettling history.

There are, after all, still far more meat-eaters than vegetarians in the world although the practice of vegetarianism is no longer idiosyncratic in Western Europe or North America. On the least generous estimate, the United Kingdom now has upwards of 1.8 million vegetarians. On a more generous estimate, the United States may have as many as 10 million.[1] This means that there are more vegetarians than Muslims in the United Kingdom and almost twice as many vegetarians as there are Jews in the United States (even on fairly liberal definition of who is and who is not Jewish). But vegetarians are still a small minority of either population, somewhere over 3 per cent of the population in both the United Kingdom and the United States. These are still substantial numbers and, if the UK data is reliable and representative, the individuals concerned are spread across the social classes although they are unevenly distributed by age and gender. Anyone over 50 years of age is unlikely to be vegetarian, but anyone under 20 has a disproportionately high likelihood of having at least dabbled with a vegetarian diet. In all age groups, there are significantly more females than males.[2] Depending upon what one thinks of vegetarianism, this may seem to reinforce the idea that, by nature or by nurture, women tend to be more compassionate than men, or that they are more prone to emotional fancy. In what follows I will incline to the view that our emotional response is worth attending to, emotions need not be placed outside the bounds of the rational, we may, after all, respond emotionally for a reason. And sentimentality itself may be understood not in terms of emotional responsiveness but as an inappropriate emotional responsiveness, in the present case, as a standing disposition to respond with pity where there is no real or significant harm. But in the case of the killing of other creatures the harm is both real and significant, and the spectacle is capable of bringing about pity on the part of anyone not desensitised by repeated daily exposure.

On this view of our emotional responsiveness an emotion may even be required if we are to fully grasp what we encounter. But emotions can also be misleading. Our difficulty is then to separate out those occasions on which emotions track the world from those on which they do not. In shaping our lives in line with an unease about animal slaughter, as many vegetarians and vegans do, they (or rather, *we*) may be succumbing to an intolerance for the actual, for the inescapable realities of life and death that are found everywhere in nature. This intolerance might be regarded as a form of puritanism that makes us ill-suited for contentment or, more simply, for being at ease in a world where the cycle of birth and death is going on all around. This is what Michael Pollan suspects.

> A deep current of Puritanism runs through the writings of the animal philosophers, an abiding discomfort not just with our animality, but with the animals' animality too. They would like nothing better than to airlift us from nature's 'intrinsic evil' – and then take the animals with us. You begin to wonder if their quarrel isn't really with nature itself.[3]

Although I am a vegan, I take it that Pollan's charge has real substance. For Pollan, vegetarians and vegans find it difficult to come to terms with the more unpleasant aspects of nature. And while it may be tempting to dismiss this whole idea of puritanism as far fetched, or based only upon isolated cases for meat-free diets that are not always well set-out or well understood, there may be something more to it.

A concept of 'puritanism' may be exactly what we need to make sense of some of the more problematic aspects of our current dietary practices. However, this line of thought can be pursued in a way that departs significantly from Pollan, who suggests that the puritanism in question (however we understand it) is, in a special way, connected to vegetarianism. But insofar as there is a real problem here, it may be more widespread. The elongation of food chains that situates the vast majority of us only as consumers, and not as producers of food, can encourage all sorts of problematic fussiness about what we eat, a fussiness that is not restricted to meat-products or to foods that are unwholesome or plausibly suspect. Here, I do not have in mind anything so well-founded as a concern to avoid genetically modified produce, or food that is laced with antibiotics and pesticide residues. I am interested, instead, in a misplaced concern with something akin to contamination, a misplaced concern that equates industrial food processing with hygiene and a natural irregularity of shape with mutation. What has come to be viewed with suspicion is, as Pollan suggests, anything too natural and unprocessed, anything with the wrong sort of history.

For example, the thought that vegetables come from the earth is not geared to endear them to a generation that equates the soil with dirt. Barbara Kingsolver picks up on this point with her characteristic good humour,

> Our words for unhealthy contamination – 'soiled' or 'dirty' – suggest that if we really knew the number-one ingredient of a garden, we'd all head straight into therapy. I used to take my children's friends out to the garden to warm them up to the idea of eating vegetables, but this strategy sometimes backfired: they'd back away slowly saying, 'Oh *man*, those things touched *dirt*!' Adults do the same by pretending it all comes from the clean, well-lighted grocery store. We're like petulant teenagers rejecting our mother. We *know* we came out of her, but *ee-ew*.[4]

This unease about food, and more particularly about the history of food, is not simply the result of the modern supermarket system. It predates the latter, and can be seen in the curious doublethink that allows at least some carnivores to dissociate their meat from its animal origins. There is a wonderful section in Proust's novel series from the early 1900s, *A Remembrance of Things Past*, that illustrates the point. Proust's fastidious narrator tells of a childhood occasion when he witnessed his aunt's house-maid chase a chicken with rage and shrill cries of 'Filthy creature! Filthy creature!' and yet by mealtime the beast had been ritually transformed into the beautiful, golden skinned presentation that graced the dinner table.[5] Proust's narrator, who is ordinarily so detailed, decides that there are some things about the past that it does not do to enquire into too closely.

This attitude is familiar. Increasingly, it is the norm among carnivores. Some can still tolerate the sight of an entire roasted pig, but many do not like to be reminded that meat comes from beings who have lived and breathed and passed through slaugh-terhouses, and had their head and feet or extremities removed. Tongue, heart, lungs and viscera are also, for many, too reminis-cent of a living origin to be present at mealtimes in anything other than an unidentifiable form. Setting aside crustaceans, molluscs and sea creatures whose lives we barely understand, chicken and fish are the only kinds of meat that still resemble the animals that they came from. And increasingly, they too are reshaped into anonymous portions. The familiar mealtime evasion that this promotes involves a reluctance to engage openly and honestly with the messiness of our world and the disturbing messiness of what must always, and unavoidably, figure in the background to a carnivorous diet. Meat-eaters, just as readily as vegetarians, may wish that their food had a different history, or no history at all, that it arrived hot from the replicator, in the manner of meals served up in the pages of science fiction.

ARE ANIMAL PRODUCTS BAD FOR US?

But even if we allow that the average meat-eater currently lives in something of a bubble, isolated off from any disturbing contact with the messy realities of their food, we may nevertheless think, with Pollan, that the charge of puritanism (however understood) has a special force in the case of vegetarianism because of the latter's strong prohibitions. Any dietary practice that involves prohibitions (on whatever grounds) may be difficult to separate out from the treatment of the natural and wholesome item in question as a source of real or figurative contamination. An obvious example of this is eating kosher. Faced with difficulties in rationalizing and justifying the practice, an appealing option is to suggest that its ethico-religious prohibitions *track* medical facts about harmful eating practices. This is not, now, the dominant view of the law of kashruth, but it has, in the past been an influential one. The great twelfth-century philosopher Moses Maimonides justified kashruth as just such a form of ethico-medical guidance, 'The principal reason why the Law forbids swine's flesh is to be found in the circumstance that its habits and its food are very dirty and loathsome.'[6]

Although vegetarians and vegans are unlikely to be happy with the idea that animals are intrinsically unclean, it may be tempting to modify the stated grounds for suspicion and to claim that animal flesh is, in some respect, nutritionally unwholesome. What may make this line of thought particularly tempting for at least some vegetarians and vegans is an aspect of their personal experience, the phenomenology or experience of what it is like to have a meat-free diet but to stumble into the meat-aisle in a supermarket, or to buy meat for a housebound relative. We are trained, from infancy, to regard certain things are bad, or dirty and not to be ingested, we are socialized into directing a visceral response of disgust towards certain things and a dietary practice can affect the way in which this response is directed. It may be tempting for vegetarians and vegans who develop such a response to meat, raw meat in particular, to suspect that their bodies are trying to tell them something, that their disgust, however mild or extreme, is there for a good reason.[7]

Accepting that we should sometimes listen to what our bodies are trying to tell us need not, in this particular case, require that we view animals themselves as a contaminant. Disgust operates with locational constraints. For example, what is inside our own bodies is not regarded as disgusting until it is *out there*. Similarly, we may at least suspect that in the case of the vegetarian or vegan's reaction to row upon row of raw meat, that the response does not pick out the uncleanness of animals, but rather the disturbingness of certain animal parts when removed from living creatures. By contrast, the roadside body of a rabbit, even with its flesh clearly exposed, may not be a source of disgust even for these same non meat-eaters. It may be a source of pity. Animal flesh is not normally regarded as vile or viscerally unpleasant just so long as it is in the place where it belongs as part of an entire creature.

Be that as it may, as long as there have been articulate vegetarians there have also been vegetarians who have been ready to play upon the visceral response to meat by linking it in a problematic way to the maintenance of physical well-being. Plutarch's equation of meat-eating with the consumption of death is a case in point.

> Can you really ask what reason Pythagoras had for abstaining from flesh? For my part I rather wonder both by what accident and in what state of soul or mind the first man did so, touched his mouth to gore and brought his lips to the flesh of a dead creature, he who set forth tables of dead, stale bodies and ventured to call food and nourishment the parts that had a little before bellowed and cried, moved and lived. How could his eyes endure the slaughter when throats were slit and hides flayed and limbs torn from limb? How could his nose endure the stench? How was it that the pollution did not turn away his taste, which made contact with the sores of others and sucked juices and serums from mortal wounds? [8]

This position is not just ethical. It is quasi-medical. The contamination that is threatened by the consumption of animal flesh is bodily. Meat-eating is presented as a form of self-harm, but the harm involved and the contamination threatened, is of a special and ambiguous sort. Plutarch (46 C.E–120 C.E) plays upon the readers' fear of death at a time when even a minor illness could be fatal. His view is one offshoot of a trend in early vegetarian thought in the West, a trend that gives force to Pollan's charge of puritanism. The same trend is exemplified in a different way by early Platonic defences of vegetarianism. The third-century CE writings of Porphyry in particular regard meat as a threat that is both corporeal and spiritual. For early neo-platonists like Porphyry, the physicality of dead animals was liable to corrupt the more spiritually entangled being of men.[9]

We may reflect more favourably upon the carnivores of Northern Europe during the same, pre-Christian times, when the mortal remains of men were deliberately mingled with animal remains, presumably in the hope of giving the deceased some of the animal's characteristic strengths in any afterlife. Familiar myths in which humans acquire animal characteristics again originate from carnivorous and pre-Christian cultures that seem utterly unashamed of their own physicality, mortality and creatureliness. This may seem to involve a higher regard for animals than we find in Plutarch and Porphyry. But it does nothing to undermine the important idea, at work in both, of a certain kind of physical complicity in harm. The consumption of meat, at least when it is not a necessary expedient for our own survival or well-being, is an endorsement of its production, and however much we shy away from a recognition of what this production involves, we are all ultimately aware that meat is not grown in-vitro or replicated into existence. A desire to avoid such physical complicity, or the legitimation of harming animals in the required ways, may be separated out from any fable that turns perfectly healthy meat into a medical contaminant.

A vegetarianism of any defensible sort may have to accept that meat is not nutritionally compromised, that it does us no physical harm to eat it (in suitable amounts, with suitable preparation and so on). Even when carefully separated off from any idea of the intrinsic uncleanness of animals, the idea that meat *per se* is phys- ically harmful is, at the very least, ill-informed. Vegetarians may be, on average, more healthy than carnivores, and less prone to type-2 diabetes or strokes, and vegetarian children may not have some of the obesity problems that affect a significant segment of young carnivores. We may even allow that, when the relevant comparison class is taken to be the idealized 'average carnivore', it is probably wiser to adopt a vegetarian diet. But this provides no good reason to regard meat-eating *per se* as intrinsically harmful. It is not, for example, obvious that vegetarians have significant health advantages over those who engage in what we might call 'best carnivorous practice'.[10]

To say this is simply to acknowledge that we have evolved to cope with meat-eating, or rather to cope with eating meat when it has been reared under reasonably natural conditions, without some of the more dangerous innovations of industrialized meat-production, and then cooked or cured. Eating raw meat is a rather different matter. A visceral response not so much to raw meat itself but to the prospect of eating it really does look like bodily wisdom. The healthiest way for humans to eat uncooked flesh is in small quantities and straight from a blender. Our digestive cycle is too quick, and our stomach muscles insufficiently robust to break it down in large quantities. We do not have the advant-ages of a more ape-like physiology.

But, when suitably prepared, and minimally processed by cooking or curing, animal flesh is not intrinsically harmful to the average human. (Again allowing that the latter is something of an idealization.) This applies even to animal fats, which have a particularly bad reputation that is rooted in popularized versions of late twentieth-century nutritional debates about lipids (roughly: oils and fats). The problem with some of these debates, or at least with the way in which fragments from the debates seeped into public awareness, is the way in which they focussed more upon sourcing than upon nutritional composition. The origin of meat is more important from the standpoint of ethics than that of nutrition, thought of in isolation, as a scientific discipline. Like so many other things (such as water and oxygen) animal fats are bad for us in excess or in poorly chosen combinations or when they are contaminated as a result of bad practices of one sort or another (in preparation, storage or rearing). They are not bad for us *per se*.[11] That meat or fat comes from animals makes its consumption ethically problematic, but does not make it harmful in the most basic of physical senses.

By comparison with vegetarianism, veganism has a better claim to track at least one medically significant fact about humans. Vegans try to avoid all animal produce and as part of this personal prohibition they avoid milk, cheese and dairy products. In this respect, veganism is within the range of diets that humans have evolved to cope with. Anatomically modern humans have been around for a great deal longer than domesticated cattle and milk extraction from livestock. Our biology predates and in many cases does not accommodate the latter. As a result, many of us are not biologically geared to cope with the lactose in milk except during the earliest years of our lives (sometimes just the first few months). Lactose tolerance into adulthood is a local and specialized adaptation that many of us do not possess.

With the exception of those with a strongly pastoral Northern European ancestry, most people in the West (and this includes most Americans) tend not to have the attractively named SNP C/T13910 gene and are to some degree lactose-intolerant after about the age of 4. From that time onwards, milk and cheese are more digestible than cardboard or grass, but only to a degree. Some parents will know this from personal and harrowing experience. Lactose-intolerance is normally a minor irritant that may never be identified. But sometimes, it can be a significant health factor, particularly when it is present during early infancy and prevents weight-gain. It is also an accelerant for the aesthetically and psychologically unsettling skin problems associated with puberty. However, going vegan as a teenager may carry penalties of a different social sort, and reduction of dairy intake may be enough to bring matters under control. It is not, in any case, the fact that dairy products come from animals that makes them nutritionally problematic. What matters, from a health point of view, is the composition of the animal product and not its origins. Human milk or synthetically produced lactose (of which there is now a great deal in a surprising range of products including some medicines) would be just as troublesome. Furthermore, animal-derived milk, with the lactose-content reduced or removed, is already available through major supermarkets. An upshot is that veganism can be a good health move, but it is by no means a requirement for good health. A balanced vegetarian diet or best carnivorous practice can be just as healthy.

A corollary of the above point about lactose-intolerance is that vegetarian diets that happen to be high in dairy (as a way to compensate for the absence of meat-derived protein) do risk being more unhealthy than familiar carnivorous diets. However, with occasional exceptions that seem to be associated with the impact of local culinary traditions (such as vegetarianism in Hong Kong, which *is* high dairy), there are no indications that veget-arians are more dairy-dependent than carnivores. Perhaps surpris-ingly, vegetarianism in the United States tends to be low dairy, and this may be due in part to the availability of a wide range of soy products in most American cities, and the ready availability of soy substitutes for milk more or less everywhere in the West.[12]

VEGETARIANISM WITHOUT PURITANISM

Acceptance, on the part of vegetarians, that meat is not harmful may erode any suspicion that they are more liable to puritanism than carnivores. But a companion charge may then be applied. Vegetarians may be caught between a rock and a hard place. If they are not puritans, they may be regarded as all too ready to compromise and not nearly single-minded enough in their pursuit of an ethical dietary practice. Hugh Fearnley-Whittingstall adopts this second and related line of attack in *The River Cottage Meat Book* and points out (correctly I would say) that the considerations brought forward by vegetarians as reasons to reject meat-eating (that it is bound up with animal slaughter and is often implicated in mistreatment) can also be applied to their own practice by comparison with veganism. (Towards which Hugh Fearnley seems to have a higher regard.) He may over-simplify when he states that 'the dairy industry and the beef industry are one and the same thing' but the integration of the two *is* extensive.[13]

This charge, which is one of stretching tolerance to the point of inconsistency, is a strong one. Most eggs are factory farmed and produced under conditions far more horrendous than those under which pasture-fed beef is reared. Chicks bred for laying within the industry are killed straight-away if they are male (gassing is one normal option); ill and exhausted hens *are* routinely killed, at the end of a short laying career. (For a long time a forced moult by malnutrition was a standard technique to temporarily restore productivity but this is now a restricted, and in some cases outlawed, practice.) If you eat eggs, as vegetarians do, then your diet is liable to be connected, in all sorts of ways, to both lifetime harm and indirectly to the killing of fellow creatures. Even if you keep your own laying hens to ensure the best of treatment you may have to be ready to put them out of their misery if a fox has been in the enclosure. How to kill a chicken is one of the first things that a conscientious owner has to learn. Besides which, it is something of a myth that adequate space alone will prevent hens from pecking each other, and the standard industrial practice of cutting off the nerve-filled beak (beak-searing) to prevent pecking is not an ethically tolerable option. A cock may be required to keep a group of laying hens in good order, but if the cock is fertile you may end up with fertilized eggs and (again) the problem of how to dispose of an ongoing supply of male chicks.

Similarly, vegetarians consume milk, cheese and dairy products. But cows have to be pregnant in order to produce milk. If their offspring is a bull calf, it will be killed immediately or else it will be absorbed back into the food chain and killed later, traditionally for the production of veal because milk cows are selected for conversion of feed to milk rather than feed to body mass. But with cross-breading this, at least, can be avoided and many bull calves are now worth rearing for beef. As for the mother, she may be well treated on smaller and more ethically informed farms but within the industrial system that supplies most of our dairy products she will normally be milked to exhaustion and then slaughtered after about 3 years. If you consume dairy products, as vegetarians do, then your diet will again be linked indirectly to slaughter.

These things are true. And considerations of this sort are usually advanced as reasons for going all the way to veganism in preference to what is sometimes rather technically called 'lacto-ovo vegetarianism'. Hugh Fearnley's deployment of these disturbing but morally relevant facts is aimed at keeping vegetarian sympathizers firmly within the meat-eating fold. After all, if a vegetarian diet is in practice still tied in some way to slaughter, then the vegetarian does not get what they want, although they may delude themselves into imagining that their diet is disconnected from significant harm. By comparison, the honest meat-eater may seem to be more in touch with the realities of their food. But this case for meat-eating depends upon two claims, one of which is stronger than the other. First, it depends upon the genuine insight that a complete disconnection from slaughter is utterly unavailable to vegetarians, except perhaps those who live a life of self-sufficiency. Secondly, it plays upon a barely concealed perfectionist assumption that separation from animal slaughter would have to be pure and complete in order to be at all worthwhile. Stated in these blunt terms, the perfectionist assumption is problematic, and it is not clear whether Hugh Fearnley subscribes to the view in question or (perhaps more likely) whether he believes that vegetarians subscribe to it. It is, in either case, a problematic view because many practices and activities that fall short of perfection still have significant worth. Cooking and the playing of music spring to mind, and smallholding too is a case in point. In the growing of produce and the rearing of animals, there is a significant difference between 'partial success' and 'complete failure'.

Unless vegetarians buy into the puritanism of requiring perfection here and now, an appeal to the imperfections of vegetarianism will not work. They can simply face up to the limits of their practice while claiming that an imperfect severing of the connection between a dietary practice and animal slaughter may still be a good thing, even if it falls short of the ideal. A different way of making the same point is to say that what matters most in this context may not be any absolute standard of consistency or perfect accomplishment, but rather the idea of progress. That is to say, vegetarianism can be thought of as a practice that is embraced by people like us, by flawed and imperfect agents for whom it is a significant move in the right direction. And this claim may have some persuasive force even if there is never any prospect of complete success or of further movement. When thought of in this restricted way, vegetarianism may still be a favoured option for obvious reasons. Its connection to slaughter is more indirect than that of meat-eating. Unlike meat-eating, it cannot plausibly be regarded as an endorsement of slaughter, after all, eggs and (vegetarian) dairy products are not themselves dismembered parts of dead animals. It remains the case that meat, rather than eggs or dairy, is at the heart of the system of animal slaughter. There can, after all, be no meat without the intentional death of some animal, but the same is just not true for eggs or dairy. Animals killed by the dairy industry and passed on from the latter to other sectors of animal-based production are usually killed because of the economics of the industry, as a matter of expediency and not because their untimely death is a product requirement.

To represent matters in the way that I have done is to suggest that vegetarians and carnivores can be every bit as puritanical as each other but that vegetarianism itself is best understood not in line with an impossible demand for purity, but rather as a matter of degree and aspiration. In support of this, it may be pointed out that vegetarianism admits of all sorts of shades and variations. Individuals intend or try to avoid meat; they may generally or mostly go for a non-meat option (because it is a non-meat option); or they may restrict themselves to eating fish very occasionally when a protein-craving strikes. They may even set out to eat no meat at all but then experience periodic 'lapses' that may indicate dietary imbalance. But it would be odd to regard individuals who fall into one of these groups as anything other than vegetarian, or, in the terms favoured by surveys of eating habits, 'mostly vegetarian'.

There are also vegetarians who, under particular and unusual circumstances, will continue to eat a dish once they realize that it contains some ingredient that a host did not think of as meat-related (such as chicken stock or prawns). They may do so where there is a danger of giving offence or causing embarrassment, just as a meat-eater may continue to eat something that they would not normally dream of consuming, for similar reasons. Again, it would be odd to think of such individuals as anything other than vegetarians who are caught up in an awkward situation. Straining the concept a little more, we may allow that there are vegetarians who permit themselves a 'Paris-exception'. In another country, on a lovely night, and unable to find anything else that is decent to eat, they may eat meat as a one-off. Even in the latter case, which involves choosing deliberately to eat meat, it would seems churlish to deny that such individuals are genuinely or at the very least 'mostly vegetarian'.

My point here is that vegetarianism is not like virginity (whatever one may think of the latter). It can accommodate compromises without being lost. Acceptance of this may be bound up with a realistic attitude to the prevailing circumstances within which vegetarians, like the rest of us, live. Our food chains are so based around meat and the by-products of animal slaughter that comprehensive and unqualified avoidance can pose difficulties of a sort that escape notice until a sustained vegetarianism is actually attempted.

Anyone who occasionally eats inadequately labelled meals from a supermarket may well intermittently consume some or other meat-related ingredient that is not so obvious as a large chunk of flesh. Anyone who buys a hot chocolate with marshmallows will (almost certainly, but unwittingly) have consumed pork or beef gelatine. The problem here, which is especially acute when eating out, applies both to vegetarians and to vegans, even though the latter have the reputation of being more 'hard-core' about meat-avoidance. Vegans do not (intentionally, normally) eat either meat or eggs and dairy produce, but it is not unusual for vegans to apply different standards of caution to the avoidance of meat and to the avoidance of other animal-derived ingredients. The former is sometimes regarded as a *more* serious matter.

As dairy produce gets everywhere (breakfast cereals, sweets, veggieburgers, all 'quorn' produce) the reliable avoidance of dairy would require a complete avoidance of processed food and this may be impractical. Vegans who consume even bread from supermarkets may risk unintentionally consuming small amounts of milk-derived ingredients, for example calcium or, again, lactose. Vegans who are affiliated to some or other dietary group will be aware of the scale of the problem. To clear matters up the Vegan Society in the United Kingdom produces a handy pocket-sized *Animal Free Shopper*, but this does not make a complete purity any more attainable. A list of E-numbers that are 'Possibly Animal-Derived' is given but the list of ingredients whose provenance is uncertain but suspect is almost exactly fourteen times as long.[14] Most UK supermarkets help out by producing their own list of what they consider to be vegan-friendly products. Waitrose, Somerfield, Spar and Sainsbury do so. But most of these products are not labelled in-store as vegan-friendly and the largest UK supermarket, Tesco, has a patchy record on collating vegan-friendly information.[15]

Part of the difficulty arises because the by-products of the meat industry can often be replaced by plant-derivatives or can be produced synthetically. This is a consideration that vegetarians and vegans may bring forward for regarding slaughter as redund-ant. Animal carcasses are not a unique source for anything that we need. But it also means that the history of ingredients, even down to the level of vitamins, may not be reliably judged simply on the basis of information that is given on the packet. To suggest this is not to lapse into a suspicion about motives. The truth does not need to be hidden away in a devious manner. In many cases, it is simply not known. It would seem odd to suggest that the food market is geared to deceive vegans because it does not seem to be geared to cater for vegans at all. They are, for the big food retailers, an afterthought, a comparatively small niche-market that is too limited in extent to merit its own in-store section.

Even for those vegans and vegetarians who try to avoid resorting to ready-meals, and who are extremely cautious about eating-out, there is still the problem of alcohol. Some super-markets carry own-brand alcohol on their shelves and their labelling policies can be helpful. Sainsbury flag up vegan-friendly wine as well as vegetarian-friendly wine. But a great deal of beer and wine (and hence food made with either) is not vegetarian. Real ale is traditionally clarified with isinglass, a form of fish-derived gelatine. Cider is arguably the safest alcoholic product to take if you want to avoid all animal-derivatives but keg, canned and bottled beers are also usually (but not exclu-sively) non-animal. However keg beers do sometimes contain chemical agents such as *glyceryl monostearate* (E471) to control foam levels. This can be animal-derived but its provenance in any particular case will be uncertain. There is little point in asking bar staff about it during the busy hours of a Friday evening. For those who want to consume alcohol that lacks explicit and reliable labelling (and this means *most* alcohol), vegetarianism and vegan-ism will be a matter of intention, aspiration and degree. Once this is understood and accepted, there is very little room left for puritanical standards.

WHAT CAN VEGETARIANS REASONABLY HOPE FOR?

Given such limitations, it is not entirely correct to say *that a veget-arian is someone who does not eat meat* or to say that *vegans do not consume any animal products*. And given this, we may ask *just what do vegetarians and vegans reasonably hope to achieve or to avoid?* As vegetarianism (and veganism too) is not a political movement with a single specifiable 'line' of response, I will try to answer the question by starting with what seems uncontroversial. I will take it that vegetarians and vegans are liable to agree that, all other things being equal, we have good reasons to eat in ways that show our commitment to the value of animals. Both are also liable to agree that this gives us good reasons to avoid the deliberate killing of animals and to reject any dietary practice that requires such deliberate killing (slaughter) to take place and any dietary practice that may reasonably be understood as an endorsement of slaughter.

But beyond this, the convictions of either group form more of a patchwork. Vegetarians and vegans do not all have definite views about animal rights much less an agreed position. Nor do they all share the view that everyone else ought to follow their own example. Good reasons for a dietary practice can be trumped by other considerations that might lead others to adopt a differ-ent practice. Vegetarianism and veganism can be (and I will sug-gest often are) regarded not as a universal blueprint for human life but as more of a contributory response to a shared human predicament. Some may hope that they are personally making a direct difference to the life-prospects of animals, and possibly to the environment, while others may hope only that vegetarians *en masse* will impact upon the level of slaughter.

Whatever we may make of the former claim, the latter looks defensible. Given the level of vegetarianism in both the United Kingdom and the United States, it is difficult to deny that it does impact upon the level of slaughter even if the impact is not enough to keep the figures from steadily rising. But this does not translate into a clear-cut impact by particular individuals. There is rarely any way in which a consumer can know just how or whether their own purchases will impact upon the further course of food production. Carnivores and vegetarians alike are rarely in a situation where there is a clear impact associated with personal purchasing decisions. With occasional exceptions, there is no clear link to the bringing about of any animal's death as opposed to the endorsement of the practice of killing. Some of the more expensive restaurants are an exception, the ones that allow diners to buy a particular lobster from a tank. The same courtesy is not extended to land animals for obvious reasons. And even the buying of a turkey directly from a farm at Yule, Christmas or Thanksgiving, an act that may seem to involve condemning a particular animal to death, is more likely to involve picking out a creature whose fate is already sealed and whose date of slaughter may not be altered.

Supermarkets make our food chains far longer than this, so long that they sever any direct and clear link between individual purchases and the incidence of killing. When someone buys a chicken or a portion of beef, the animal is already dead and the purchase does not automatically result in an extra animal being killed in order to restock the shelves. The market is too insensitive to the actions of individuals to respond in this way. As a result, it is possible that someone may have been buying meat all their life but may have had no impact at all upon the total number of animals killed. Conversely, it is an inconvenient truth that vegetarians cannot divide the annual number of animals slaughtered by the total number of carnivores to arrive at a ball-park figure for how many animals they have personally saved by abstaining from meat. The world is not so transparent. Supermarkets restock as a matter of routine, or, when they are more information-sensitive, they restock when a threshold of sales has been reached. An upshot of this is that there can, from time to time, be what we might call the 'threshold chicken' or the 'threshold steak pie' whose purchase does trigger reordering, and the reordering can trigger other actions, including slaughter. But 'threshold' items are the exception.

This has, from time to time, been brought forward as a reason for not being a vegetarian or a vegan. Why become vegetarian when this personal decision may make no difference? If a single individual does not eat meat, the world of meat-rearing will still roll along and will probably do so in exactly the same way. It will not make any difference to the livestock, but the individual in question will have sacrificed his or her own pleasures for nothing. Here again, we have a line of thought that represents vegetarianism as a sacrifice, rather than treating it as a life-enriching and expressive dietary practice. But let us grant that the actions of the individual vegetarian or vegan may not improve the fortunes of livestock in any way. And let us set aside the important idea of contributing to a collective impact, an idea that seems at home in discussions of diet. After all diets place us within a tradition, they are shared ways of doing things. Even so, with our focus upon the isolated individual, it can still make perfectly good sense to be a vegetarian. What is missing from the focus upon the sum total of animals killed, is the personal dimension of morality, and the question of whether we ourselves have killed them or have in some way gone along with or endorsed their killing.

An extreme case may allow us a glimpse of what is at issue. Let us suppose that you are out on the ice with a group of seal clubbers. A seal stands before you. You know that if you do not club it then somebody else will. You may even have tried persuasion and you may know all too well that persuasion does not stop seal clubbers when their blood is up. In this situation, you still

have a reason not to club the animal, even though the only difference in the outcome will be a personal one, the difference will
be that you do not become a clubber of seals, although this may
not make you feel any warm glow of self-satisfaction. You may
even feel disappointed that you could not do more or bring
about an outcome of a different sort. My point here is that we
have reasons to avoid being the person who causes or endorses
harm even when we cannot prevent the harm from taking place,
and even when we cannot in any way diminish its extent.

Even so, there is a significant difference between buying or
consuming meat and a more direct involvement in slaughter,
whether under relatively humane conditions or under the reck-
lessly savage ones that figure in the above seal-clubbing scenario.
With direct involvement in slaughter, there is always a definite-
ness about harm that is absent in the case of simply eating meat.
But the eating of meat still requires that the intentional killing of
some animal must have taken place and is, thus far, an endorsement of its killing. Vegetarianism and veganism do not require
such intentional killing to have taken place, and practitioners of
both may reasonably hope to minimize any personal connection
to it. In doing so, they express their appreciation of the value of
other creatures.

Here I speak of minimizing a connection to harm rather than
removing it entirely and of 'intentional killing' rather than 'killing'
per se. Diets that are aspirationally meat-free or, in the case of
vegans, completely animal-free, still do require the death of animals.
Complete purity is not and never has been an option, even for
vegans. If someone was fortunate enough to avoid all slaughter-
related ingredients of whatever sort, and to remain connected
to slaughter only in other ways (e.g. through taxation and the
paying for farm subsidies, or through commerce generally), they
would still have to eat grains and pulses. And while food is
grown in the soil and has a more or less natural history, there will
always be a blood price to be paid for a harvest. The numbers of
animals inadvertently killed through harvesting can be reduced

with caution. Field margins can be increased and harvesting can start in mid-field and work outwards. This may help (views on what is best differ), but the taking of animal lives cannot be entirely avoided. Recognition of this is a matter of acknowledging that the presence of we humans as part of our planetary eco-system, is always, to some extent, at the expense of other creatures. And this is one of the many things that vegetarians, vegans and carnivores have in common.

4   Diet and Sustainability

DOES *LOCAL* TRUMP *VEGETARIAN?*

What kind of people do we need to become if we are to have a tolerable and sustainable future? One part of the answer may be that we need to become the kind of humans who are better at relating to the non-human than we have been in our recent past. We might even say that we need to become a part of the land-scape, a feature of our locality rather than something more akin to a mining engineer determined to rip out the means of sub-sistence from the body of the earth. This latter way of putting matters involves a figurative way of writing but it situates locality as something important. And this may seem to be the right thing to do. But locality can be a point of contention between vegetarians, vegans and carnivores. For vegetarians and vegans, a disturbing feature of meat production is that it takes place nearby, not exactly on our own doorsteps but at no great distance. The locality of harm, and our awareness of it, may seem to provide additional reasons for trying to avoid those foods that require the harm to take place. But considered from an ecological point of view, the locality of livestock rearing and of slaughter translates into savings in energy and carbon emissions that would other-wise be required for transportation. By contrast, non-meat staples such as rice or pre-packed salads are often shipped or flown-in from elsewhere, sometimes under refrigerated conditions. This can be a wasteful process. It gives rise to what we might call the locality critique of vegetarianism.

It may be tempting here for the vegetarian to claim that their refusal to eat locally produced meat is part of a legitimate trade-off between animal interests and broader environmental considerations. But if we hold that re-establishing a sustainable environmental balance is our most fundamental priority, as well we might, then the terms of this trade-off may seem problematic. The broader environmental considerations should surely trump animal well-being. On a rather different tack, it may be pointed out by the determined vegetarian that the only kind of reasoning in play here is consequentialist. We are looking at the costs and effects of rival dietary practices and not the practices themselves. Attention is given to the results of meat-eating and a veil is drawn over the, often cruel and unavoidably harmful, processes that lead up to these results. Perhaps we should not be in the business of pursuing good outcomes in bad ways. After all, some ends may not justify the means by which they are secured.

Given that the environment matters, the vegetarian may go on to point out that the existing livestock system is itself far from a pastoral idyll. The era of locally grazed cattle eking out their limited days in short-term security and leisurely contentment is, for the most part, gone. Livestock production is an integral part of an industrialized food system and like all industry it has a tendency to pollute. Land is overstocked and overgrazed; waste products from livestock are generated far in excess of requirements for manuring; and excrement runs off into waterways and rivers. Antibiotics used routinely to keep intensively reared cattle alive long enough to reach their slaughter-weight work their way into the soil and again into the water system. These processes take place to the detriment of the regular-sized creatures, bacteria and microbes that have traditionally kept the rivers and soil in a healthy condition. It is tempting to think that, on closer inspection, vegetarians need to make no appeal to a trade-off between animal interests and the environment, and that what would serve both is a significant curtailment of industrialized livestock production.

This is a temptation that we should perhaps resist. Unlike appeals to meat tasting too good to give up, or animals being too dumb to matter, the locality critique appeals to concerns of a deep sort, and to a readiness to accept what is required rather than what is convenient or habitual. To do justice to its merits, let us assume that its priorities are appropriate. Let us assume that we are terrestrial creatures in a more fundamental way than we are meat-eaters, vegetarians or vegans and that if the well-being of the environment currently requires us to be carnivores, then we should be carnivores. Here I frame matters in terms of environmental well-being and not in terms of an ideal of eco-logical perfection. I will take it that, from an ecological point of view, we are not called upon to be perfect but to try and live in a sustainable way.

I will also assume that the most pressing of all environmental problems is global warming and the emission of greenhouse gasses that fuel this warming rather than pollution of other sorts. Given time, and perhaps a little help, the earth's depleted and poisoned soil may heal itself. But time to heal is exactly what global warming threatens to deprive us of. As a contributor to these harmful processes, the emission-requiring energy-use involved in the transportation of non-meat foodstuffs may strike us as a luxury. A diet that *requires* remote sourcing may then seem to be well-intentioned but, from an environmental point of view, too expensive to be borne. As Catherine Osborne points out, in her ecologically minded critique of vegetarianism, 'If our concern is simply to procure an adequate diet with minimal trouble, minimal expense, and minimal sensual indulgence, there seems no reason to reject animal products. Rather the reverse.'[1]

An extreme case may illustrate her point. What are we to make of the vegetarian who lives in Orkney, an island cluster just off the northeast coast of mainland Scotland? Orkney is a remarkable place but not the warmest location in the world and not a prime

site for growing vegetarian-friendly produce. The Orkney vegetarian would require a good deal of their food to be shipped in,
and by sourcing their food in this way they would be shunning an
obvious local food source, that is meat.[2] A similar point is made
by Michael Pollan with reference to upland areas and thin soils
in the Unites States, 'The world is full of places where the best, if
not the only, way to obtain food from the land is by grazing (and
hunting) animals on it – especially ruminants, which alone can
transform grass into protein.'[3] The point could also be made with
reference to at least some coastal areas.

Here, it is important to remember that most of us are not
living in such locations or on thin-soiled uplands. Perhaps isolation does give some reason for meat-eating, but it is a reason that
most of us do not have. Even so, in saying this I may be in danger
of missing the point: the more extreme cases of isolation may
be indicative of a problem faced by anyone who wants to justify
a vegetarian practice that is kept afloat on a sea of transport-
generated carbon emissions. The point is not obviously wrong,
although it has more force in the United Kingdom where agricultural production is limited by climate and land availability, than in
the United States. The United Kingdom has an entrenched import
dependence when it comes to food. It is a smallish island, towards
the colder end of Europe, and has a relatively largish population.
Compared to the rest of the world, it *is* Orkney. Non-meat foodstuffs are routinely sourced abroad.

What the United Kingdom is exceptionally good at is over-
producing cereals (barley, wheat and oats in particular). It is less
effective at producing legumes (oilseeds such as soy and pulses
such as chickpea or kidney bean). Vegetable cultivation has been
somewhat neglected in favour of these cereals, and domestic
fruits have declined in popularity with the arrival of a much smaller
cluster of imported varieties. Organic food comes in for a good
deal of criticism in this regard, even from ecologically minded
commentators such as James Lovelock, because the demand for
organic in the United Kingdom far outstrips domestic supply.[4]

Roughly half of the United Kingdom's organic produce has to be imported. But the sourcing of *non-organic* vegetables and, especially, fruit is similarly poor. About 30 per cent of all vegetables and more than 90 per cent of all our fruit is sourced abroad.[5] The attention given to organic imports can therefore be disproportionate. It can obscure the generally poor state of domestic production when compared to our high levels of consumption.

Without either a population reduction or a major change in tastes, the United Kingdom is neither geared nor equipped to be a self-sufficient agricultural producer. While this may lead us to say that vegetarians have no special case to answer, we might instead look at matters in a different way and suggest that by shunning any major foodstuff that is domestically and, even better, locally available, they make an already bad situation worse. A presupposition here is that going vegetarian or vegan really does make a difference. And so, criticism of this sort rules out an appeal to the quite different consequentialist argument that individuals do not impact upon the level of slaughter.

Be that as it may, the US case is, in several respects, different. Favoured by climate and by geographical expansion, it has historically been a net exporter of foodstuffs to other parts of the world. And the range of its produce is far greater than the range of UK produce. Oranges and rice can be sourced from California and need not be brought in from Spain or from the East. Unlike the United Kingdom, the United States is also a major soy producer. Generally, it is better equipped for self-sufficiency, although the country is so large that buying domestic is not necessarily the same as buying local. Moreover, the historically stable pattern of a US trade surplus in food produce is steadily giving way to a deficit. The change is not primarily driven by vegetarians and vegans (as in the United Kingdom their numbers are too small to dictate matters) but it *is* largely driven by the import of non-meat items, so the vegetarians and vegans may again not be helping matters. According to the United States Department of Agriculture (USDA), by 2002 the United States was importing only about 5 per cent of its animal products but it was already importing over 19.1 per cent of it crop-based products.[6] Whatever else is driving demand, we might be tempted to suggest or concede that meat-free diets are part of the problem.

Alternatively, as the US imports tend to be fruit, vegetables and certain kinds of pulses rather than grains, it is tempting to say that vegetarians are getting matters (roughly) right. Everyone ought to eat more of these healthy foodstuffs. If they are available domestically that's good, but if not then remote sourcing may be a price that is worth paying. Health reasons are unlike other, more trivial, reasons for energy use and carbon emissions. Besides which, the knock-on environmental effects of ill-health on a vast scale could be dramatic: more heating, more car journeys and (under a market system) high financial costs that need to be funded by economic activity which may itself turn out to be an environmental burden. In an indirect sense, keeping healthy can be a way to be environmentally friendly.

We may also have reasons of a different sort to buy remotely sourced goods from countries with a colonial past or with a record of being pounded on the world marked by long-standing and protectionist European and American agricultural policies. We may have good reasons to balance up past wrongs and the purchasing of foodstuffs may sometimes be an effective way in which this can be done. But once allowances for personal health and historic justice have been made, the case for local sourcing kicks in and diets become difficult to defend if they push up food imports or if they further an already import-dependent food culture. As inhabitants of countries with a major responsibility for global warming, it may be argued that we have a special reason to overcome scruples about eating meat if it allows us to eat more locally.

And so it has seemed to a number of individuals and organizations. Alongside carnivores, vegetarians, vegans and freegans (whose *bête noir* is supermarket waste), there are now locavores whose principal aim is to eat locally produced food. Roughly, this equates to food produced within a 100-mile radius but the distance can vary depending upon how strict a locavore one wants to be.[7] At an institutional level, the most notable expression of this claimed primacy of the local is the Slow Food Movement, originating in Italy in 1989, and founded by the journalist Carlo Petrini, with the aim of protecting local food traditions in much the same way that wildlife conservationists aim to protect indigenous species. According to the Movement's website, their goal is 'to counteract fast food and fast life, the disappearance of local food traditions and people's dwindling interest in the food they eat, where it comes from, how it tastes and how our food choices affect the rest of the world'.[8]

The movement claims 100,000 members in over 133 countries. These are not big numbers when compared to the population as a whole, or when compared to the number of vegetarians or vegans within it. But the Slow Food Movement promotes community and, in the face of the version of cosmopolitanism offered by McDonald's, Burger King, WalMart and Tesco, this may seem to be a welcome development. A further indication of the revival of local food traditions is the resurgence of farmers markets, scarcely in existence in the United Kingdom or the United States only two decades ago, but now re-established in most urban centres. Even some of the supermarkets have tried to temper their corporate images by incorporating small amounts of local produce on their shelves. Given the ecological importance of local sourcing, there is a case for the practising vegetarian to answer, although here I will restrict my attention to consideration of energy-use and emissions rather than any communitarian dimension of the charge. After all, vegetarians may not eat local meat, but it is far from obvious that they lack community spirit.

A more restricted locality critique of vegetarianism involves a single-minded focus upon transportation. The very idea of transportation catches our attention in part because, unlike the great industrial emissions, it is something that we can, up to a point, personally control. We can choose to drive less often, or to drive a smaller car, or to take public transport. But this focus may obscure the larger contribution to energy costs and emissions that occur elsewhere in the food chain, before and after food is moved around. According to one study conducted at the end of the 1990s and quoted favourably by Peter Singer and Jim Mason, roughly 29 per cent of the energy costs of food in the United States goes on processing and a further 26 per cent on home preparation. Only 11 per cent of the energy costs goes on transport.[9] And even this single figure for transport is misleading. It is foodstuffs that are transported by air or that require refrigeration (such as leafy salads with a short shelf life) that are particularly energy-expensive. Food that is shipped and does not require refrigeration, such as bananas, or anything that ripens gradually *en route* or at the destination, can be a relatively energy-efficient source of nutrients in spite of distant sourcing.

Part of the reason for this is that products sourced outside of countries such as the United States or the United Kingdom are often *not* produced using our own energy-hungry technologies. Many farmers in the Third World simply could not afford the equipment, the expensive fertilizers and the hit-and-miss pesticides that are now standard in the West where the dominant buyers, the supermarkets, insist upon scale and continuity of supply irrespective of season and source. The upshot is the prevalence, and heavy subsidizing, of systems that are extremely energy-expensive. In Florida and California, for example, local tomatoes and rice are available in good quantities but locality does not automatically equate with eco-friendly. To hit the shelves at the right time, tomatoes are often picked green and ripened on ethylene gas. Similarly, although 95 per cent of the rice grown in California is produced within 100 miles of the State Capital (and is local by the *locavore* standard), it can be more energy-efficient to ship it in from the East because of the energy-expensive Californian systems of production.[10] It may be no coincidence that the USA Rice Producers' Group has been a prominent opponent of climate change legislation. Its members would have a good deal to loose if such legislation became effective. It would hit production in places such as California, although perhaps not as much as worst-case scenarios might lead us to expect.[11] The Californian case supports Peter Singer's overall view that 'proximity to the place of production is not necessarily a reliable guide to energy savings.'[12] Even so, we may suspect that meat is a different and rather special case.

WHY MEAT PRODUCTION TENDS TO BE ENERGY HUNGRY

There are some forms of meat production that are effectively what Joel Salatin and Michael Pollan call 'grass farming' or, a variation of the latter, what is better known in Europe as 'biodynamic farming'. Under such systems, animals are let loose on pasture and then periodically moved around to prevent overgrazing and to help fertilize the soil. The animals are then harvested once they are large enough to eat. This is an energy-efficient system of production and it is eco-friendly at ground level. Grasses such as clover are used to help fix nitrogen in the soil without the use of chemical fertilizers, and these grasses get most of their energy from the Sun. But few farmers in the United Kingdom or the United States operate in this way. Biodynamic farming has traditionally been big in some areas of Europe but in the United Kingdom it is a small fragment of an organic sector that by 2003 still accounted for only around 4.4 per cent of our total farmland.[13]

Meat production more typically involves only a component of putting animals out to pasture. Cattle are mostly fattened up on grains and not on grass. Insofar as grass figures at all, it does so shortly after calving and later on in the silage (usually fermented ryegrass) that is produced using some of the same energy-expensive systems as grain production. Although grass itself is cheap, from a farming point of view there are commercial advantages to rearing livestock on more expensive feeds such as soy and maize mixes. Above all, animal feeds allow stocking levels to be determined by the market and not by the extent or declining quality of the land. With the addition of growth hormones to the feed, a much larger animal is also produced.

There are numerous problems with this dominant system. An obvious one, for anyone who is a champion of locality, is that animals fed on grains are not truly local. The European Feed Manufacturers Association estimates that the EU livestock industry imports 77 per cent of its feed requirements. In the case of soy, it mainly comes from Brazil and Argentina.[14] In the United Kingdom, the Department for Environment Food and Rural Affairs (DEFRA) is busy doing what it can to change matters. Programs to promote domestic pulses and oilseeds are encouraged.[15] But currently, animals with a large soy component in their diet are the end result of global systems of production. British poultry may be every bit as tasty as patriotic advertising suggests, but it is, for the most part, converted Latin American protein. Poultry in the United States is a rather different case. Domestic production of soy and maize is extensive. But the United States embraces genetic modification in a way that its more cautious Canadian neighbour and European countries have not. It is, in this respect, a source of a different kind of environmental concern.

But even if livestock feeds in the United States were produced on an entirely domestic basis, this still would not make standard or statistically normal and average forms of meat-eating more eco-friendly than the average vegetarian diet, given that feed crops are in most instances produced using chemical fertilizers. Without going into excessive detail, the key to making an artificial fertilizer is ammonia distillation. The conversion of ammonia into nitric acid and then to nitrates to be mixed with phosphorous and potassium, to make a standard fertilizer base, is a straightforward process. But it is the ammonia itself that is the difficulty. Producing it depends upon superheating gasses under pressure and superheating does not come cheap, either in cash terms or in terms of the energy involved. It is so expensive compared with more traditional systems of sustaining soil fertility that the entire process has to be heavily subsidized by governments, making cheap food something of an illusion. It is paid for through taxes rather than at the checkout but it is still paid for. The upshot is a grain-production system in Europe and America that is driven by demand for livestock feed, which depends heavily upon government subsidy, tolerated debt on the part of farmers, and a massive ongoing supply of fossil fuels, oil in particular to supply the energy to fix nitrogen in the fertilizers. As well as being energy-expensive, it also compromises the idea of locality. Grain-feeds are only as truly local as the energy that is used in the fertilizers required to produce them.

This overall situation could, at least in theory, be tackled at some time in the future if we were to develop high-yield strains of genetically modified crops (rather than the current poorly performing strains); and if we were to substitute these for a significant part of the imported component of animal feeds; and if we were to use fertilizers whose nitrogen was fixed by using energy from nuclear power. But this conjectural package, which demands only technological change rather than any alteration in consumer activity, may seem to be a rather high price to pay so that our generation can have its fill of meat.

Vegetarians and vegans also eat grains and pulses, some produced domestically and some imported in the form of soy. Whether or not these foodstuffs are imported, they may also be produced using the same energy-expensive artificial fertilizers that are used to produce animal feed. However, far less grain ultimately goes into feeding the average vegetarian than goes into feeding the average carnivore. The reason for this concerns proteins, the building blocks for body growth and maintenance. Vegetarians get their protein, and the constituent parts of protein (amino acids), from non-meat sources. Carnivores get protein components from these same sources but they also get complete proteins directly from meat. But meat production depends upon a system of protein-components-in and far-less-protein-out.

As well as protein that is simply not absorbed but is excreted, livestock animals need a substantial bone-structure, hoof, horn and all the body parts that we don't eat. This is where a good deal of the nutritional content of grains and soy ends up when it is fed to livestock. Some of this can be recycled in various ways but much of it is straightforwardly lost.[16] Feeds also have to sustain animal movement and that involves energy loss of a more straightforwardly unrecoverable sort.

We may then wonder why humans ever farmed animals at all but the answer to this is simple. Some nutrients are difficult to access or to process (such as the acorns that pigs love to eat). But more fundamentally, we lacked any other way to access the nutrients in certain kinds of grasses. Cattle can eat what we find indigestible. They have a rumen, a second stomach in which grasses can ferment. The simple model of cattle eating grass and humans then eating cattle is an efficient solution to tap into the available natural resources. But once cattle are fed on grains and pulses instead of grass or difficult-to-access nutrients, that is on foods that humans can without any great difficulty eat (and enjoy and be creative with), meat production becomes grossly inefficient. It involves waste on a scale that could only be supported as a form of luxury production, which is exactly what most contemporary livestock rearing is. The only merit of meat produced in this way is that it continues to supply us with complete proteins and relieves us of the daily burden of having a more varied diet. Contemporary meat-eating may not be a dietary formula for gluttony but it is a formula for a certain kind of dietary laziness that has little in common with the meat-eating of our ancestors.

Most cattle are now pastured only during the earliest stages of their brief lives. In the United States, after a short sojourn on the grasslands, beef cattle are normally reared in Concentrated Animal Feeding Operations (CAFOs) that are also known as feedlots. As soon as practicable, they are moved off of grass, corralled together in large numbers in noisy and dusty pens, and fed a diet of grains and pulses laced with antibiotics. Because pulses are (in some cases) part of the natural diet of ruminants, but grains are not, stomach problems ensue. Levels of activity are compromised and a variety of digestive illnesses are a constant threat.

In the United Kingdom, everything is much smaller. There is nothing quite like the CAFO system. But even so, the same pressures to *get big or get out* have been at work. So, for example, since the 1970s the smaller domestic breeds of cattle have tended to be replaced with much larger European breeds that are then kept under cover for much of the year. Cattle reared indoors can have a more controlled grain-heavy diet. The system is less forced than in the United States, and routine disease is less rife, but even with some revival of grazing and domestic cattle breeds such as the Hereford and the Aberdeen Angus, meat production remains heavily grain-dependent.

The result of having grain-fed cattle is that those fields of wheat, barley and (increasingly) maize that we see during summer are not, for the most part, destined directly for human consumption. According to an article in *Time* magazine, by the start of this century US livestock was already consuming five times as much grain as the human population, but in this respect the United States is unusual because of the amounts of meat in the average diet.[17] Just how much of the nutritional value of the animal feed is lost in the process of conversion to meat, or how much ends up as something that humans cannot eat or (at their own peril) should not eat, varies depending upon a number of factors. The most important of these is the kind of meat that is produced. Meat quality and protein density is not uniform, but the sheer bulk of grain that it requires may give some indication of the loss involved. At the lower end of estimates from the United States, 13 lbs or less of grain-based feed can now be converted into 1 lb of beef. This may sound like an under-performing system of conversion, but it is working more or less flat-out. As a process of protein conversion, it is a dramatic improvement upon the system that was in place a couple of decades earlier. But it is still enormously wasteful.[18] The figure for pigs is more impressive. They are, roughly, twice as efficient at protein conversion. Around 6 lbs or less of grain can produce a single pound of edible pork.[19] Chickens are super-efficient and by a generous estimate from the world's largest chicken producer, *Tyson Foods*, for every 2 lbs of feed they are able to put on 1 lb of flesh.[20] However, that is a live-weight figure. Once we allow for the blood and water lost upon death, the ratio may be closer to 3 lbs of grain to 1 lb of flesh.

Given the relative efficiency of poultry at converting feed to meat, it is little wonder that meat production, marketing and consumption in both the United Kingdom and the United States, has tended over time to shift away from the carnivorous paradigm of red meat and towards intensively farmed chicken. It is now the single most regularly eaten meat in both countries. Even so, the most productive conversion systems in use still involve somewhere between one- and two-thirds of the nutrients that are fed to poultry being written off as waste, as a loss that is built into the conversion process. It does not take any complicated maths to figure out that humans eating foods based on these same grains and pulses, with some suitably limited processing, is a good deal more energy-efficient than sourcing proteins from grain-fed animals.

But it can take some complicated aggregating of data, and some controversial methodological assumptions about how best to do this, in order to quantify the global environmental benefits of vegetarianism or veganism. The UN's 2006 report *Livestock's Long Shadow* attempted to do this and claimed that the livestock sector was responsible for around 18 per cent of greenhouse gas emissions.[21] This has become a popular figure for newspapers to cite when they carry articles on food and the environment. Crucially, it places livestock production as a larger greenhouse gas polluter than *all* transport (and not just food transport). This implies that the environmental advantages of vegetarianism could be considerably greater than any advantages of the most local systems of meat-eating. It is also a claim with radical and (for some) alarming, policy implications, the most obvious of which is that we produce far too much meat and should cease to do so on anything like the current scale. The reaction to the report by cattle ranchers and their political allies has been predictably hostile. A rule of thumb here seems to be that if you do not like the idea that human activity is a prime cause of global warming, then you will be even less fond of the idea that meat-eating on an industrial scale is a major contributory factor.

But there is a difference between these two cases. In fairness to the critics, because of the complexity of aggregating the data, the evidence for all transport being outstripped by the livestock sector alone is *not* as clear-cut as the evidence for the human contribution to global warming. Few things are.[22] But on a more low-level comparison, one that sets aside global impact in favour of a focus upon the diets of individuals, meat-eating still turns out to be environmentally problematic in a way that most forms of vegetarianism and veganism are not. The standard starting point for such a low-level dietary comparison is currently Eshel and Martin's 2006 study of the energy use and carbon emissions required by various standard forms of diet. What they found (or claimed) was that poultry consumption is relatively more benign in terms of emissions than beef consumption. (A predictable result.) But they also suggest that it could require a lower level of energy and emissions than lacto-ovo vegetarian diets that have a high or even standard dairy component. However, they note that such diets may be uncharacteristic for vegetarians. (Studies for the United States usually show that vegetarians tend to have a low dairy intake. They draw components from a vegan diet and use plant-based dairy substitutes such as soy.)[23]

If correct, what this shows is what we might in any case expect. There is a crossover at the upper end of energy-hungry vegetarian diets and the lower end of familiar carnivorous diets. But the standard US meat-heavy diet, which has around 28 per cent of animal sourced food, has no comparative advantage over the average vegetarian or vegan diet. And when compared to a completely animal-free (vegan) diet Eshel and Martin's calculation of the energy impact is that the standard US meat-eating diet requires and extra 1,485 kg of carbon dioxide emissions per person, per annum. If we find the temptation to quantify on a grander scale utterly irresistible (as Eshel and Martin do), this aggregates out as an extra 6 per cent in the level of US greenhouse gas emissions.[24] This might not be enough to convince meat-eaters to reduce their own carbon footprint by becoming vegetarians, but it does support the view that vegetarianism and veganism are, in comparative terms, eco-friendly.

ECO-FRIENDLY DIETS

This does not mean that *all* carnivorous diets are eco-unfriendly. Here and there, pockets of traditional, ethical and alternative farming survive and cater for a strong segment of the food market but require below-average levels of energy input.

Most obviously, there are grass farmers (who rely on pasture and try to restrict or cut out grain-feeding) and there are producers of organic meat, ranging from the producers of non-organic who want to occupy this niche as well through to farmers who want to work exclusively with natural processes at the cost of accepting seasonality. And there are biodynamic farmers associated with organizations such as Demeter, who are ethically driven, who extend the systems used by grass farmers and who strive to integrate inputs and outputs to eliminate waste and bypass the need for energy-expensive animal feeds, fertilisers, pesticides and regular doses of antibiotics.[25] But this entire sector is small in comparison with the mainstream of meat production. Demand for the product often outstrips supply and, in the case of organic, consumers can still, in many areas, only access it through the supermarkets and anything sold in the latter may be regarded with a degree of scepticism.

However, in the case of livestock a guaranteed difference is built into the certification systems. The main organic certifiers in the United States (the Rodale Institute) and in the United Kingdom (the Soil Association) will only certify meat if the grass component of diet is high and the chemical additives are minimal. The Soil Association sets the bar much higher than the EU standards for organic and will only certify beef if 60 per cent of its diet consists of grass, hay or silage. Organic cows can still be finished more or less intensively, in barns and away from pasture, silage can still be energy costly, and the remaining 40 per cent of the feed can come from cereal sources, but this is still a significant constraint upon the prevailing intensive system's reliance upon grain-based feeds and industrial chemistry to build body mass. Insofar as this 40 per cent is made up of grains, it is still enormously wasteful in terms of protein conversion, but relative to the norm, it is far more eco-friendly.[26] Organic cattle, as a result of certification restrictions and ethically driven practices, also tend to have a smaller body mass, so organic cuts tend to be more expensive, promoting what may be regarded as a better dietary practice. Meat may not be intrinsically bad for us, but too much of it certainly is.

Grass farming, whether certified as organic or not, is even more pasture oriented than organic systems, although it lacks the same complex certification process. This can make it difficult for consumers to know just how much of the feed is grass and what else the cattle have been given. Consumers can, of course, buy directly from farms but half a morning's drive to secure a small amount of meat can start to pile up the energy costs. To ecologically minded farmers in the United States, people like Joel Salatin in the Shenandoah Valley, grass farming has seemed attractive because of the way that some organic production is compromised by a tendency to mimic standard industrial practices and to operate only as a form of input-substitution (change the feed but keep everything else pretty much the same).[27] Complex organic certification systems can also be seen as surveillance and may leave small producers vulnerable to a sudden loss of license. However, grass farming tends to be small-scale as well as labour-intensive. Salatin is its best known champion in the United States, but he farms on only 100 acres of pasture together with a larger area of forest. Michael Pollan, initially a supporter of organic, but in more recent years a critic, takes the smallness of grass farming as a mark of its higher level of integrity.[28] He may well be right about this but farming with a mixed system on such a small amount of land ends up focussed upon grass for the cows. Other animals fare less well. Poultry and rabbits end up confined or caged in order to protect the land and maximize the soil conditions. Moreover, scale is a genuine issue when the feeding of millions is at stake and it is organic farmers who have done most to try and address the problems of scaling up and of shifting urban consumers away from the most ecologically damaging forms of meat.

Given the continued use of substantial amounts of grain in the finishing of livestock (and the consequent large-scale nutrient loss) there is, of course, no good reason to think that a diet containing meat, but only limited amounts of it, produced according to regular organic standards, is more eco-friendly than a vegetarian or vegan diet even if the latter does contain more fruit and vegetables, and even if some of this has to be remotely sourced. But a limited-meat diet where the meat is more or less exclusively sourced in the locality and produced using only biodynamic or grass farming techniques, or organic techniques of the best sort, may well be more eco-friendly than vegetarianism, especially in cases where practitioners of the latter are fond of out-of-season produce. However, those who are in the best position to pursue a carnivorous diet of the most eco-friendly sort are small producers and members of rural communities that have a significant small-producer component and a high level of food awareness. Individuals in these circumstances have a reason to eat meat that most of us do not have. Even so, given that vegetarianism and veganism are still relatively eco-friendly, it need not be thought of as an over-riding reason, but rather as one reason to set against others (such as the desire to avoid a dependence upon harm).

To make this point, as a concession, is not to concede much, or indeed anything that has not been known for some time. The maximal eco-diet is unlikely to be vegetarian or vegan. It is, instead, liable to be the kind of diet that survivors of an ecological disaster, or castaways on a remote island, would be forced to adopt. This would not be a vegetarian diet but one whose ingredients were produced by small-scale mixed farming with small numbers of pasture-reared livestock. To ensure the most efficient use of the grass available, dairy production might also have to be limited. (After all dairy cows have to maintain their own body mass *and* produce milk.) Anything liable to upset the fine tuning and integration of such a system would result in a non-maximal outcome and, in a 'survivor' scenario, could lead to failure. I present this observation as a rough and ready point, as something that is intuitively obvious. But, if needed, some experimental evidence is also available. When experimenters, at the School of Health Sciences at the University of Wales in Cardiff, set out to devise the maximal eco-friendly diet they followed the initial assumption that a vegetarian diet would be best. It does, after all, have good eco-friendly credentials. But they quickly abandoned this approach on the grounds that the diary component turned out to be a problem.[29]

Perhaps they lacked imagination. People often assume (wrongly) that vegetarians are high dairy rather than low dairy. But we need not make any ungenerous assumptions of this sort to recognize that the Cardiff study may well be right in its assumptions. A cautious, locally sourced, low-volume meat diet, with meat produced using modified forms of traditional methods, may well yield a better approximation to the maximal diet. Putting a small number of animals onto hilly grasslands that are unsuitable for cultivation, and then slaughtering them once they reach a suitable weight (preventing them from consuming just to sustain bulk) has always been an energy-efficient way to source proteins that would otherwise remain inaccessible. Given this, it is easy to see why a vegetarian diet, although eco-friendly, is probably not as good as it gets.

This point has been seized upon by some critics of vegetarianism who think that an evaluation of its merits is best made by comparison not with standard carnivorous diets but with the most ecologically sensitive ones, no matter how limited their availability. This is the line taken by Michael Pollan and Catherine Osborne's treatment of vegetarianism also depends upon just this kind of contrast:

> The vision of simple local self-sufficiency, uncluttered by worldly concerns, as recommended by Epicurus . . . is clearly easier to realize in a traditional farming system, where producers live off whatever their own land is able to produce and do not need to engage in trade and commerce.[30]

But it is not only critics of vegetarianism who have picked up on the limits of its environmental credentials. Even though environmental considerations (alongside health reasons) figure prominently among stated reasons for being vegetarian, the prominent American vegan campaigner, Erik Marcus, has downplayed appeals to both, suggesting that 'the vegetarian movement would do well to reduce the attention it gives to health and environmental concerns . . . these arguments need to be made with great care and they should be tailored to specific food choices and diets.'[31] His overall point is that an appeal to the environment will work only against particular features of the prevailing meat-production system and not against meat production *per se*. However, Markus may be in danger of surrendering too much ground too easily. It is not obvious that the environmental benefits of vegetarianism depend at all upon how well it compares to carnivorous diets that very few people actually practice. And while there may be a need for caution when generalizing about the advantages of vegetarianism (and a failure on the part of some vegetarians to think in terms of considerations such as seasonality), there are counterbalancing dangers of other sorts. There is just as much danger that the sheer possibility of an eco-friendly carnivorous diet may be used as a stalking horse to provide dubious justification for widespread carnivorous practices that are not nearly so eco-friendly as their practitioners may assume.

5   The Impossible Scenario

UNIVERSAL VEGETARIANISM

The ready availability of a healthy vegetarian diet may lend plausibility to an ecological charge, one that turns availability into a threat rather than an opportunity. So long as vegetarianism is a minority activity, all well and good, but what would happen if all or many of us were to become converts? When Catherine Osborne writes that 'a great deal of complicated commercial exchange would be necessary to support a purely vegetarian economy for more than a part of the population' she articulates this reasonable concern.[1] Such a situation would be radically different from our current predicament. As radically different, it is also easy to imagine that it could be damaging in ways that our existing set-up is not. The very language of vegetarianism requiring 'support' suggests that it would be burdensome, although the extent of the burden is not clear. An extreme scenario that may be imagined along these lines is one in which an entire society, or a nation, or a group of nations such as the UK or the EU, undergoes a transition to vegetarianism or to veganism. Pollan refers to just such a scenario as a 'vegan utopia' and (predictably) disapproves.[2] He suspects that a universal abandonment of meat-eating would be a disaster and even vegetarians and vegans might suspect that he could be right.

But it is not obvious that this should matter in terms of how we act now, as individuals living in a predominantly carnivorous culture. There is, after all, no immediate prospect of a mass abandonment of meat. There is no threatened dictatorship of the herbivores. It may also be suspected that many vegetarians simply have no determinate view about whether or not everyone else ought to turn vegetarian. Organizations are a different matter and they do tend to hold positions on this issue. But when asked *why are you a vegetarian?* individuals may (and often do) reply without appeal to anything akin to a universal human obligation. And we may readily understand just why this is the case. What we might call 'universal vegetarianism' is not a basic requirement for human well-being or sustainability. If we ask the question *what kind of people do we need to be if we are to have a tolerable and sustainable future?* it is unlikely that our best answer will be *vegetarians*, although a significant level of vegetarianism could perhaps contribute to such a future. So, in the absence of any proselytizing zeal or evangelical fervour on the part of vegetarians (and vegans), it is not always obvious why some defenders of meat-eating think that there is a problem here.

One reason may be the influence of an idea of moral egalitarianism that stems from the eighteenth-century German philosopher Immanuel Kant. In one way or another, all contemporary philosophy is influenced by Kant and so too is a good deal of our intellectual culture. But the particular influence in the present case is the idea that defensible moral principles must provide universal and impartial guidance. On this view, if it is right for me to hold and act on some moral principle, then it is right for everyone else to do so. The presupposition here is that morality has rational underpinnings and rationality turns out to be the same for all of us. This is one way of making sense of the idea that our humanity involves us a shared moral predicament. But not everyone agrees with this approach, or with the way in which Kant places emphasis upon what is universal and shared rather than emphasizing the importance of responding to the particular and to unique circumstances. Even so, let us accept, for the moment, that there is something in what Kant says. This would still not, on its own, generate a problem for vegetarianism (or for veganism which, after all, might be regarded as an extension of vegetarian dietary practice). But if we hold to a confused version of Kant's position, then we may find a problem where there is none. And this is just what some otherwise excellent commentators on food ethics have done. Even Colin Tudge (a defender of ecological livestock rearing who views vegetarianism as a useful contribution to restoring ecological balance) cannot resist the temptation of a misplaced appeal to Kant, 'Vegetarianism does not, then, and cannot, provide what we ought to be looking for: a system of farming that would suit all of humanity (and our fellow creatures) for all time.'[3]

Stepping back a little from the heat of controversy, we may see that this is a very odd thing to say. After all, there are few important practices that all humans could adopt, even for a short period of time and on a local scale, without chaos ensuing. If, for example, we were all to become doctors society would collapse. But it is important that a minority of individuals do so and some of these individual really could have a duty of this sort. Similarly, it is a pleasure to write this book but I also have a duty to do so, given that I promised to write it. But nobody else has this same duty. My own duty stems not so much from a universal and shared human circumstance but from a particular sequence of historic events that help to mark out my life as distinct from that of others.

Above all, Kant was not claiming that everyone ought to act in exactly the same way, but rather that we all ought to act upon the same background principles. And this might result in different actions by different individuals in different circumstances. Sometimes more than one course of action may be defensible. Let us suppose that we all ought to act in line with an appreciation of the value of other creatures. This seems to be an intuitively plausible claim, although Kant's own views on the matter are complex. He tried to give animals their due but regarded our relations to them as practice for the real thing, for carrying out our duties with regard to other humans.[4] Be that as it may, one individual might turn vegan because they accept, as a point of principle, that animals are due consideration, while others might accept the same principle but act upon it in a quite different way. It may even be intelligible that, given differing circumstances, the individual in question could *only* act in line with the relevant principle by turning vegan, while some other group of humans, faced with different circumstances, could have a much broader range of options. The different circumstances in question might involve the local availability of defensibly produced meat, the vital needs of the individuals in question and the affordability of produce. Expense could place a diet out of reach for the poor but not out of reach for the affluent. Under such circumstances, the affluent *could* have a duty to become vegan, but the poor would not.

Failure to allow for this is a failure to do justice to how flexible a Kantian approach can be. Accordingly, vegetarians and vegans can argue, along broadly Kantian lines, that we are all subject to the dictates of exactly the same moral principles and these moral principles require people in one type of situation to stop eating meat, while allowing that those in some other situation may have sufficient reasons for continuing to do so. A (broadly) Kantian vegetarian might allow that meat-eating is defensible (and even a duty) for a hunter gatherer, but not defensible for a bank clerk who has readily accessible alternatives to eating meat. More straightforwardly, a vegetarian or vegan might simply reject a Kantian framework and argue that an appeal to duties and to universally shared background principles can make sense of only a part of our moral life. There are, after all, moral reasons beyond those of duty and beyond any appeal to general rules or principles. For example, it may not be my duty to act in a particular way in some unusual situation for which there could be no obvious background rule, but it may still be a good thing for me to do so.

DOES MEAT-EATING MAKE VEGETARIANISM PRACTICAL?

Setting aside any appeal to an oversimplified Kantian position, Catherine Osborne and Michael Pollan regard the impracticality of universal vegetarianism or universal veganism as a symptom of a deeper problem. If I had to sum up the suggested problem briefly, I would do so by stating that, in some sense, vegetarianism is a luxury, and a luxury of a particular sort. To get to the roots of this matter, let us consider a parody of an ancient dietary practice, associated with affluent Manicheans, adherents of a religious tradition in competition with the mainstream of early Christianity. The Manicheans did not believe in a universe created by a single benevolent god but in a fundamentally dualistic universe, a cosmos torn in every respect between the good and the bad and, according to St Augustine, they favoured a version of veganism. Let us suppose now (by way of an exaggeration) that some of the more elevated practitioners of this religion had extended their dietary restrictions to avoid any compromise with the bad. Let us suppose that they would not even compromise with the harm involved in picking fruit from any living thing or the harm involved in cutting short the life of plants. Instead, when left to their own devices, they would wait until the fruit fell or the seeds were scattered, or, more probably, they would hire servants to accept the supposed fault and then happily enjoy the benefits.

Not everyone could have adopted such a practice. And here it does seem to be a damning indictment of it that it could not have become universally practical. Without men and women prepared to get their hands dirty, it would have resulted in wholesale starvation. The impracticality of making this lifestyle universal genuinely is a symptom of the way in which it would have had to depend upon the very practices that it rejected. If contemporary vegetarianism and/or veganism is dependent, in a similar way, upon the continuation of a widespread carnivorous practice by others, this might count strongly against it. Any claim that meat-eating is morally problematic by comparison with vegetari-anism would be undermined. Particular individuals might still have good reasons to become vegetarians, but only so long as others afford them this luxury by getting their hands dirty and remaining carnivores. (Here we also have a recurrence of the charge that there is something vaguely puritanical about meat-free diets.)

I will take it that this is what at least some advocates of ethical meat-eating are getting at when they focus upon the apparent impracticality of universal vegetarianism. Their point is not that animals do not matter, but that we need a widespread practice of meat-eating and the explanation for this necessity usually involves some appeal to ecological considerations. Some variant of meat-eating has, after all, been necessary in the past. Hunter-gathering groups could survive through periods of dearth, their dietary flexibility allowed them to do so, but sooner or later they required periodic and significant inputs of meat for at least some of their number in order to keep going. And even in medieval times, the monastic vegetarianism of the few could not have been spread successfully across the countryside and into the towns. It was an elevated practice that rested upon the actions of more worldly meat-eaters. And perhaps meat-eating is still a social necessity from which only individuals can have the privilege of opting out. Considerations of this sort matter. At the very least, they give force to the point that the old slogan *meat is murder* is based upon a very weak analogy between a practice that we outlaw and a practice that we cannot readily and comprehen-sively suspend.

But even if we did require a continuation of a widespread practice of meat-eating, this would not, on its own, show that vegetarianism is a luxury. After all, it is conceivable that ecological harm would also ensue if there were universal meat-eating, if the tens of millions of vegetarians worldwide, not just those in the West but those in countries like India as well, were to suddenly abandon their existing dietary practice. We may regard our current predicament as one in which a shifting balance exists between meat-eating and vegetarianism. A wholesale swing either way could result in problems. To say this would still allow us to point out the ecological advantages of vegetarianism for individuals and even of majority vegetarianism. It may, after all, be the case that the present balance is not the best that we can manage.

Such a way of looking at matters would no doubt be rejected by the determined advocate of meat or of meat-eating under ethical conditions. Their background assumption may be that a carnivorous diet is not only necessary to maintain some kind of ecological balance, but it is also necessary in a way that the persistence of vegetarianism is not. And here, it must be said that the numbers are stacked on the side of the carnivore. It is, perhaps, easier to envisage doing without the minority practice than it is to imagine doing without the meat-eating norm.

Barbara Kingsolver, a one-time vegetarian and then convert to ethical livestock rearing, describes herself as 'fundamentally allied with a vegetarian position in every way except one'. For Kingsolver, animals matter but so too does their meat and their other products. She has pictured the chaos that would ensue if universal veganism was to be tried even on a small and local scale. Responding to the proposal by a vegan movie star for a safe-haven animal ranch, she has some sharp and incisive comments to make. A ranch with cows and chickens freed from the shadow of slaughter would still be a place where animals would have to be milked. It would also quickly be over-run by 'an endless chain of uneaten lives'.[5]

Here the objections are admittedly provisional and their remit is set by an ill-thought-out television interview. Perhaps there would not be an endless chain of uneaten lives. The breeding of animals is, after all, something that humans are relatively good at controlling just so long as they are prepared to take the necessary and unpleasant steps. These might be disturbing to vegetarians, to vegans and even to some carnivores but they may be pre-ferable to a continuation of slaughter. Similarly, milking for the animal's own sake, to prevent mastitis, is a very different matter from milking for the sake of humans and keeping a cow more or less continuously pregnant throughout its short adult life in order to do so. But I do not think that these provisional and off-the-cuff objections exhaust Kingsolver's case. She is directing our attention to more than one type of problem. On the one hand, she attends directly to difficulties of a logistical sort to do with practicalities and detail; on the other hand, she alludes to problems of a non-logistical and deeper sort that concern the sustaining of a genuinely natural life cycle, a cycle of birth, flourishing and death.

The more mundane and logistical problems are: first, those associated with the running of an enclave of veganism in the midst of a sea of meat-eating, and second, the problems associated with any sudden transition to vegan practice, given that we would then, at the very least, have to reckon with a large number of already-existing animals. These problems are real enough. With permanent corralling ruled out, some domesticated livestock could perhaps be released into the wild or, if not exactly the wild at least into intermediate controlled zones with some monitoring and assistance, and they might fare relatively well, at least for a time, and this time might, on average, exceed that of their expected lifespan on a farm. Pigs are an obvious example of the kind of robust creatures who are capable of semi-independent living.

Other animals would fare badly. Existing programmes to 'reintroduce' animals to the wild tend to fail. Domesticated livestock would probably not thrive any better without further selective breeding for hardiness, and even then a massive reduction in their numbers might be required to prevent the rapid spread of disease and simply to offset competition for limited resources. On the other hand, there are parallels here between the prospects for animals and those for cognitively impaired humans. There was a time, not so long ago, when it was believed that they too were better off in centrally administered institutions. Their potential for a degree of independence was underestimated. But even without reflecting upon this parallel, what makes the logistical problems of an end to meat loom large may be the prospect of a sudden transition. In fairness to veganism and more particularly to vegetarianism (which is, after all, less demanding), it should be pointed out that sudden transitions can be debilitating and damaging simply by virtue of their suddenness. Any attempt on the part of everyone to engage in the best carnivorous practice, from tomorrow onwards, and to eat only the most ethically produced meat, could also bring about chaos and disorder. What would we do with all of those factory-farmed animals? Would we wait for them to succumb to disease and illness, as many of them surely would? Such creatures, after all, are not bred to last. Would we postpone any decision until the problem died? Considerations of this sort may suggest that the problems of a sudden transition are nothing at all to do with the merits of *any* dietary practice. They are to do with our own lack of patience and preparation.

So let us consider what the impact would be if a universal abandonment of meat-eating came about in whatever gradual and whatever minimally disruptive manner we might wish. And, contrary to the emphasis placed by Pollan and Kingsolver, let us focus upon the dietary practice of vegetarianism rather than veganism for the obvious reason that it is the more plausible of the two unlikely scenarios. Again, what we are looking at is whether or not at least one of these scenarios *could* be made to work. The claim that it *ought* to be made to work is an entirely different matter and it is not obvious that any argument could demonstrate so strong a claim. Both scenarios may also strike us as so unlikely as to be virtually impossible, but I will suggest that the most fundamental obstacles to a universally vegetarian society are likely to be political rather than anything to do with the requirements of ecological balance. If we allow that the politics and economics of the future may be rather different from our own set-up, then the scenario of an ecologically balanced universal vegetarianism may not be impossible at all.

Moreover, if universal vegetarianism were a practical ecologically defensible option, even if an unlikely one, it would serve to counter Kingsolver's deeper concern, the concern that anything meriting the title of a natural cycle of life will have to require meat-eating. Unlike the logistical points made above, this concern is deep because it is bound up with the kind of concern for a tolerable and sustainable future that may be an indispensable part of any adequate, forward-looking ethic. To say this implies, that Kingsolver is correct to hold that ecologically minded vegetarians and ecologically minded carnivores have a great deal in common. Both care in non-instrumental ways for the natural world and for the non-human creatures who, together with ourselves, form a part of it. But Kingsolver's worry that vegetarianism is liable to violate the natural life cycle and to cause ecological damage, although deep, may nonetheless be misplaced.

THE ECOLOGICAL PROBLEMS OF UNIVERSAL VEGETARIANISM

The idea that universal vegetarianism would unavoidably harm the planet should not be dismissed out of hand, even by committed vegetarians or vegans. It has a certain plausibility about it if we think that universal vegetarianism would inevitably be technocratic or executed along futuristic lines. I am tempted here to appeal to the way in which H.G. Wells (a notorious vegetarian) envisaged the future, although Wells rarely said what is attributed to him; or even to Lenin, who was not a vegetarian but did once remark that his new society would be a combination of soviets (workers committees) and electrification. We may, with hindsight, be sceptical about the idea that good will, solid organization and unbounded technology can solve all of our problems. In retrospect, twentieth-century modernism, and its love affair with technology, showed a good deal of contempt for any idea of a natural life cycle, and a technocratically inspired universal vegetarianism might require something along the same lines. A dependence upon conditions of stability maintained by wide-spread meat-eating might be replaced by a dependence upon an intensified form of the most ecologically suspect features of our existing systems of crop production.

Let us suppose that science in the form of industrial chemistry managed to replace seemingly outmoded ways of producing food that relied upon old fashioned animal husbandry. And let us also suppose that the resulting system continued to depend upon the soil and upon the use of vast tracts of land as a convenient growing medium in the absence of endless laboratory space. Universal vegetarianism would then be a refinement of existing and damaging trends that have led cereal production to steadily and harmfully triumph over the grazing of animals on pasture. What survives of the complexity of the countryside and of its more remote reaches might, under such a technocratic order of things, be reduced to a patchwork of monoculture fields, stamped down onto the landscape irrespective of the prevailing local conditions.

This scenario is more or less what Michael Pollan envisages, at least for outlying areas and marginal land.

To give up eating animals is to give up on these places as human habitat, unless of course we are willing to make complete our dependence on a highly industrialized national food chain. That food chain would be in turn even more dependent than it already is on fossil fuels and chemical fertilizer . . . and fertility – in the form of manures – would be in short supply. Indeed, it is doubtful you could build a genuinely sustainable agriculture without animals to cycle nutrients and support local food production. If our concern is for the health of nature – rather than, say, the internal consistency of our moral code or the condition of our souls – then eating animals may sometimes be the most ethical thing to do.[6]

Barbara Kingsolver goes international to make the same point:

> Many of the world's poor live in marginal lands that can't support plant-based agriculture. Those not blessed with the fruited plain and amber waves of grain must make do with woody tree pods, tough-leaved shrubs, or sparse grasses. Camels, reindeer, sheep, goats, cattle, and other ruminants are uniquely adapted to transform all those types of indigestible cellulose into edible meat.[7]

Kingsolver and Pollan speak from a background of knowledge. The America experience should perhaps teach us a lesson about the indiscriminate if enthusiastic stamping of crop production down onto unsuitably thin soils and rocky regions. We need only think of the dustbowl agriculture of the 1930s, when exhausted and badly eroded soils across the Midwest ruined the hopes and lives of an entire swathe of the rural population, as well as inspiring literature such as Steinbeck's *The Grapes of Wrath*, to realize that some land is just unsuitable for the sustained growing of crops. We may use it for meat production or dairy farming or else allow it to drop out of the agricultural system altogether. But if significant marginal and upland areas are taken out of production, if they are not, for example, used to pasture animals destined for slaughter, there will be pressure to increase productivity elsewhere to supply alternative sources of protein for our expanding human population. And the simplest way to do this, at least in the short-term, may be through the familiar system of chemically based agriculture, complete with energy-expensive artificial fertilizers, GM (genetically modified) crops, monocultural production, and so on. That is, through systems that have a track record of boosting productivity or in the case of GM crops (which have a dubious productivity record) through systems which hold out some prospect of boosting productivity in the future.

Faced with this concern, a determined advocate of vegetarianism might be tempted to bite the bullet and to suggest that we can improve our technology to the point where familiar problems simply vanish. This argumentative move may seem overly optimistic or naïve. At best it may show a McCawber-like insistence that something is bound to turn up, even if it is a move that could be made while diplomatically accepting that, in the past, there have been mistakes, and that modern scientific farming methods have unavoidably been subject to teething problems. While this would give the defender of universal vegetarianism a way to respond. It is unlikely to prove an attractive option to those who wish to hold onto any ecological credentials.

An ecologically minded defender of the practicality of universal vegetarianism may have to accept that any further extension of single-crop, monocultural production, in whatever cause, could turn out to be less of a utopia than a dystopian disaster or 'farmageddon'. Such a way of farming crops causes harm but it is a harm that may not be noticed unless we look down at and into the soil. We miss a good deal of what matters about the land and soil if we treat it in the manner of industrial chemistry as an inert growing-medium within which the main active components of fertilizers (nitrogen, potassium, phosphorous) do all the real work. We may see more of what there is to see if we look to ideas from ecologists who hold with Aldo Leopold that 'healthy land maintains itself as an organism', an organism with needs and requirements that industrial chemistry simply does not meet.[8] To clarify this point, the damage threatened by a technocratic vegetarianism can be specified in a little more detail. First, and most obviously, there would be the damage to the soil itself. In order to stay healthy, soil needs, at least intermittently, to carry a variety of grasses whose root systems reach down to different levels. These root systems help to support a wide variety of bacteria, microbes, insects and worms all of which do their part to aerate the soil; to build up a rich layer of plant-supporting humus and to hold and release nutrients at the right time, when they will do most to support life above and below ground.

Considerations of this sort favour ecologically informed mixed farming, with cattle grazing on the land because the evolution of cattle has, historically, been bound up with soil health. Cattle are ruminants, grassland animals, and as long as they are kept on the move at reasonable intervals to prevent overgrazing (a role traditionally performed by predators but now performed by humans), they can help to ensure that no single grass species proliferates at the expense of others. More straightforwardly, they help to fertilize the soil through the obvious processes: cows drop cow pats and so on. Whatever we eat, healthy crop-rearing soils will need at least intermittently to have ruminants grazing upon them in significant numbers.

Faced with this interconnectedness of mixed farming and soil health, a determined defender of universal vegetarianism might be driven to accept that there really is an ecological problem, but then to suggest that this is an occasion on which ecology and animal interests conflict, and that it is legitimate to side with the interests of the animals. While this is a more attractive option than outright denial that there is an ecological problem, it may become less attractive in the light of a second kind of damage that a technocratic universal vegetarianism might inflict. The establishment of universal vegetarianism at the expense of an extension of the prevailing monocultural crop systems could be a comprehensive disaster for wildlife. Steven Davis, the professor of animal science at the Oregon State University, has made this point forcefully by drawing attention to the extensive, if inadvertent, killing of animals in the process of harvesting crops.[9] Davis has gone as far as to argue that a principle of causing *least harm* to animals might well require us to eat large herbivores because crop harvesting of whatever sort unavoidably results in the killing of a much greater number of wild animals. Small creatures, such as mice and voles, loose their lives during the harvest and afterwards as a result of the ensuing loss of ground cover. We should also take into account the large number of creatures killed more directly through the use of pesticides. Wild birds are a prominent and well-known example and have been for more than half a century now.[10] Not to mention the danger to bees that results from the use of chemical agents which attack the neural systems of insects. (And when we harm the honeybees we damage a vital link in the life-bearing capacity of our ecosystems. Unlike livestock it is crucial that their numbers are not reduced.) Davis estimates that a system of meat-eating based upon mixed farming, and with animals reared on pasture, would be the approach that is geared to minimize animal harm. This suggests that vegetarians who want this same harm-minimizing outcome may be well-motivated but going about things in the wrong way.

AVAILABLE DEFENCES FOR UNIVERSAL VEGETARIANISM

Once we accept that there really could be an ecological problem, the vegetarian may attempt to tackle it by appealing to a ready-made ecological solution, that is population reduction. With a significantly reduced human population, all sorts of problems would be less intractable. There would be no pressure to increase crop productivity to make up for the absence of meat. And pointing out that this is something of a catch-all ecological solution is not in any way meant to suggest that it would be a bad move. It may turn out to be the case that population reduction is a key requirement for any ecologically defensible and sustainable system of farming.

A familiar concern about population reduction is that it may be rather misanthropic, it may seem to require widespread human harm. But it need not be seen in this light. A steady reduction of the human population to a level that placed fewer demands upon agricultural production would not obviously harm existing humans, the human species or future generations. We do arguably have an interest in having offspring, but the overall flourishing of humanity cannot plausibly be equated with our sheer numerical proliferation without any regard whatsoever to the conditions under which humans have to live out their lives.

However, the likelihood of any major population reduction may be every bit as remote as the likelihood of universal vegetarianism. For political authorities in the West, especially those who face elections, the policy is a non-starter. Encouragement to keep family size down tends not to be given for fear that it would be portrayed by opponents as an attack upon the family unit (which it is not). But it would take surprisingly little to achieve a significant overall population reduction. If we peg life expectancy at some reasonable level (and stop trying to find ways to live to infinity and beyond), and if each parent has *at most* two children and preferably one (so that nobody misses out), population levels would automatically and substantially drop. And they would do so in a manner that is in keeping with a liberal rejection of compulsion but which would, controversially, require a more open attitude towards birth control and abortion than the prevailing attitude in either the United Kingdom or the United States. Again, some imagination is needed to think that enough people would abide by this approach, even if given significant positive incentives to do so. So let us allow that there might be some good reason to expect that population levels just will not go down, and that we would understandably be loathed to adopt any measures designed to force the issue. Let us, rather ungenerously, allow that universal vegetarianism would unavoidably have to deal with this inconvenient reality.

The defender of universal vegetarianism could then play their trump card by pointing out that vegetarianism is *less* land-hungry than existing carnivorous practices. It might not be the maximal ecological option (which will always involve at least some meat-eating, given that grass-reared meat is a renewable resource) but, when compared to standard carnivorous diets, it could reduce the area of cultivated land that is required in order to support the population (whatever size that population happens to be at any given time). Because the vast majority of the nutritional content of grain is lost when it is used as animal feed, actual meat-eating (as opposed to a practice based exclusively upon the eating of grass-reared livestock) requires considerably more land-use for cereals and pulses than we need. Even without a reduction in population, universal vegetarianism might not introduce any additional pressures to engage in more intensive chemically based farming. All other things being equal, it could reduce such pressures and allow for land release.

As far as the interests of wildlife go, the benefits of any such land-release could be significant. The biggest problem for non-domesticated animals is, after all, not predation but their loss of habitat, of grasslands, woodlands, marsh and wilderness. It may not be too late to do something about this. Land quickly reverts to a condition in which farming is unpractical, but where its colonization by other creatures is virtually unstoppable. If, as a result of dietary shift, we were in a position to allow even a small portion of the land that is currently farmed to return to woodland, this would be a strong ecological point in favour of such a shift.

A qualification here is that if universal vegetarianism did free up land that was previously (and unsuitably) cultivated, it might not free up as much land as we might desire. It would make sense to convert some land over from cereal to domestic fruit and vegetable production to reduce the ecological impact of transportation. Universal vegetarianism might also require more cultivation of crops for textile production to compensate for a declining supply of leather. On the other hand, a continuation of some revised system of dairy farming that severed its current connections to slaughter for meat, but continued to harvest both wool and hides, could help to limit any additional requirements for textiles and this would be a definite advantage. It would be a controversial option, but might be regarded as an integral part of the construction of a *genuine* contract of nature, a system in which both humans and animals benefit from farming and benefit to a degree that outweighs any drawbacks.

An obvious objection to this conveniently pleasing and speculative scenario is that political systems radically unlike our own have now become almost unthinkable. And if a vegetarian utopia were constrained by the practice of *politics as we know it* then any land freed up by the end of meat-eating would *not* be taken out of regular human use. It would be used for housing, or kept neat and beautified (at the expense of the soil), or used for retail facilities, or kept under well-mown grass and planted with statues of important public figures. Even so, a reduction of the human demand for cropland might at least relieve the pressures to eat ever further into the areas of uncleared land in other parts of the world, most obviously, in the rainforests. Beef from recently cleared rainforests may be taboo even for fast-food outlets, such as McDonald's, but the land that is cleared there is mostly planted with soy and this goes directly into the food chain, some of it to feed vegetarians, vegans and carnivores in the West but most of it again goes to feed livestock. Soy from Brazil is a staple of animal feeds throughout Europe. Anything that we can do to end this contribution to equatorial deforestation would be worth considering.[11]

There is also something unsatisfying about an appeal to political obstacles as the ultimate ground for claiming that universal vegetarianism would be impractical. Any change may appear impractical once obstacles of this sort are envisaged. But it may always be suspected that a lack of imagination is being used to justify the status quo or, in the present case, a widely favoured and habitual dietary practice.

UNIVERSAL VEGANISM

In its defence, universal vegetarianism would at least have the advantage of being able to use marginal lands for the grazing of dairy animals, and more generally, the advantage of permitting a restricted system of mixed farming. Dairy farming does, after all, allow animals to perform their important traditional roles of grazing and manuring and while it has historically been connected to slaughter, the connection is contingent upon industry norms and the existing economics of farming. Some extensive system of subsidies might be required to sever the connection but food production is already subsidized up to the hilt, with a good deal of the money eventually finding its way to the major retailers (supermarkets), the fertilizer suppliers (petrochemicals corporations) and landowners who rent out their property rather than working it themselves. The change required by universal vegetarianism might include subsidies to support some on-farm livestock whose contribution could be restricted to grazing, manuring, wool and (upon death) leather. There is also no reason in principle why bull calves or other animals (goats and sheep) would have to be destined for slaughter. What we did with their bodies once they died of natural causes would be another matter. They might help to support a significantly reduced population of cats and dogs who have more reasons to eat meat than we do. The problems here are, again, political, logistical and to some extent, economic. This is not a state of affairs into which we could drift in a *laissez-faire* manner. (Without population reduction universal vegetarianism and anarchism or the dubiously named free market might not be a workable combination.) It would require at least some support, co-ordination and intervention on the part of the state. But a transition from economic support for meat-producing to economic support for universal vegetarianism would not be a move from economic rationality to irrationality. At worst, it would be a move from one kind of heavily subsidized beneficiary (petrochemicals, supermarkets and landowners) to another (the animals themselves).

The problems facing universal veganism would be far greater. Again it is worth remembering that those who adopt veganism on ethical grounds are not automatically committed to the view that everybody else should follow suit. Even so, a problem for an ecologically defensible universal veganism (a problem that universal vegetarianism would *not* have) would be the sourcing of soil nutrients in sufficient quantities. Pollan suspects that this would be an insurmountable barrier because healthy soil needs compost. However, the problem here may simply be a matter of good taste and cultural taboo. There is, after all, an obvious and all too abundant source of waste materials that we do not compost but which our ancestors were all too ready to use, a source which was still in use in parts of England in the nineteenth century when waste from London was transported out into the countryside much to the relief of the towns. It was still used extensively in China in the early years of the twentieth century, to help feed a vast population, and the practice forms an interesting contrast with current industrial alternatives.[12]

The problem, as with any compost, is to make sure that it is properly 'cooked' to kill off pathogens. (It takes about a year to do this in the case of human waste.) And if we want to integrate our cities back into a productive role in some other way than through the supply of industrially produced chemicals then we would perhaps be wise to start doing this just now, even without any prospect of an end to meat-eating. A major obstacle to progress on this matter is the existing livestock system which over-produces poor quality waste, a mixture of urine and solids laced with antibiotics that we would do well to keep clear of both rivers and soil. The high water content also makes it difficult to use in a controlled manner.[13]

More serious difficulties for universal veganism would arise if it was combined with the keeping of pets. Pets *can* be fed on a vegan diet, but we may have concerns that, in at least some cases, it would be rather forced and unnatural to do so. Again, many vegans treat their diet as a specifically human response to our history and our ongoing practices of animal harm. They do not seek to force their own response upon other creatures. But without the dairy animals that a vegetarian utopia might allow (and some 'harvesting' after a natural death), it is difficult to see where a regular ongoing supply of pet food with a meat component would come from. A society of vegans might then be required either to feed pets on protein substitutes or to live with a significantly smaller population of pets than a mixed vegetarian/vegan society would allow. Land-use under conditions of universal veganism might also turn out to be significantly greater than under universal vegetarianism. More crops with fibrous qualities, such as cotton or hemp, might be needed for textile production, in the absence of anything other than an opportunistic harvesting of wool and leather. There would, after all, be no regular and extensive supply of either from dairy animals.

In the absence of radical population reduction, and the greater flexibility that the latter would allow, a vegan utopia might genuinely pose more ecological problems than we could cope with. And so there may be some case to answer about whether veganism is a practice that needs to be supported by the widespread presence of at least one other form of diet. But this other dietary practice need not be meat-eating. It could just as readily be vegetarianism. And this might reinforce a tendency to think of veganism as a particular and relatively demanding form of vegetarianism. Be that as it may, if the availability of veganism requires only the existence of a practice of widespread vegetarianism, then neither are ecological luxuries, neither are covertly dependent upon humans continuing to rear and consume meat.

6   Love for Pets

Towards the end of the summer of 2009, a peculiar human-interest story hit the press. A primary school teacher in Kent, England, had allowed her pupils to raise a lamb as a pet, under the name of Marcus.[1] When Marcus was sufficiently grown, he would be slaughtered and his meat would be auctioned off to raise funds for the school. The process would serve the double-role of fund-raising and education. In particular, the children would learn something important about where their food came from. The teacher in question was directing her attention towards exactly the kind of thing that governments and various ethicists have identified as a major problem with modern food chains. They have become too long and lack transparency. As a result, informed choice (as well as safety information) is compromised and an evasive attitude towards meat is encouraged. To underpin food safety and restore the possibility of informed choice, sellers need to know where failures have occurred and consumers need to have at least some knowledge about what they are buying and perhaps also some knowledge about its environmental cost and what its likely health impact is going to be.

While the rationale for raising and slaughtering Marcus was clear enough, there was nevertheless an outcry. To carnivores and vegetarians alike, it seemed bizarre that someone would think it appropriate to give young children a pet and then slaughter it for meat. Part of the concern was, no doubt, concern for the children and not for Marcus. The prospect of their distress was not to be borne. Exposure to unpleasant facts can be premature. We would not, after all, allow extremely young children to see what goes on in a slaughterhouse for fear that they would be psychologically scarred. Childhood encounters with death can, after all, be terrible, and the fact that the death in question was the death of an animal rather than a human relative may be beside the point. It is the fact of death that disturbs. Moreover, the experienced death of some animal may become bound up with subsequent attitudes towards the death of humans. Horror films for adults, such as *The Silence of the Lambs*, play upon an awareness of just how this can happen.

But a desire to protect infants from the premature acquisition of disturbing knowledge may not completely account for unease with the Marcus case. After all, children are raised on farms all the time (albeit in declining numbers) and we think nothing of this. We may even believe it to be a wholesome upbringing compared to the urban and suburban norm. Such children will see the new lambs in the spring, watch them grow, and may even help to rear the weaker ones indoors. The prospect of some distress may seem to be a price worth paying for this kind of life-enriching contact with other creatures. And such a life comes with its precautions against a hurtful attachment. Children on farms, and adults too when they try to escape to the country, are usually warned (unsuccessfully) against giving names to animals who are destined to be slaughtered. Even the giving of *pastiche* names, of a sort that we would not give to humans, can begin to blur the line between treating another creature as part of a herd and becoming attached to it as a pet. And wrenching though it is for children to learn about death as an unavoidable part of livestock farming, it is not a kind of knowledge that is obviously damaging.

Part of the unease, bordering upon outrage, in the Marcus case was more specifically bound up with the fact that an animal was deliberately cast in the role of a pet who was to be slaughtered. And this we may take to be an extreme and dreadful form of harm that we do not usually inflict upon our pets. Compared to other non-human creatures, pets are accorded a privileged standing, they are regarded as having a special claim upon us, but it is not clear exactly what that claim is or why they have it. They are not exactly citizens, with clearly defined rights of participation in the public arena (something that pets would have no use for) but neither are children. And children are still community members even though they cannot participate as citizens.

This comparison between children and pets may itself be unsettling. The inclusion of pets within the ranks of *our group* may help to explain unease about the slaughtering of Marcus. But it is at best an uneasy inclusion. Roger Scruton writes of the standing of pets as honorary, 'When we become attached to an animal, we see it as an individual and as a result we lift it from its species being.'[2] Mary Midgley is more generous and suggests that 'All human communities have involved animals' and that we should regard ourselves as members of a 'mixed community.'[3] But the latter does not follow from the former. And it may be difficult to invest too much in this idea of a mixed community, given that, by familiar standards, communities require not just a sharing of history, interests and moral norms, they also require some recognition and ongoing awareness of it. When extended to include non-human creatures, the concept of community can become strained. Yet, the awareness of shared interests and the norms that emerge out of a shared history need not be the possession of all community members. And it is intelligible that we *could* live as members of a mixed community. Humans have arguably done so in the past, in the days of hunter gathering. But we may do well to place greater emphasis here upon the way that Midgley speaks of *their* inclusion in *our* community. It is a human community and they are in the midst of it. And this may remain a plausible description even if, aspirationally, we regard a true mixed-community as something to be accomplished and built (or rebuilt) rather than something that is simply given.

SHARING OUR LIVES

Even so, while we do not have a genuine pre-established mixed-community, we do, very conspicuously, share our lives with our pets.[4] And there is more to this idea of sharing our lives than spending time with them or looking after them. Care staff in experimental institutions do as much. And farmers too do the same. But there is an important sense in which the former relate to animals as benevolent warders while the latter do so as property owners. What is involved in sharing our lives is a far more personal entanglement than this. And it is the addition of this deeply personal element that may help to account for why it seemed dreadful to many carnivores that Marcus, once fully grown, was sent to slaughter, and that this was done in spite of the many offers to save his life.

However, the predicament of Marcus was, in all sorts of ways, non-standard. Pets are not normally shared around among a large group. They are usually attached directly to individuals or to families and attached in a way that gives some force to the claim that they are family members. Their ambiguous position in a human-dominated world is one where they belong at best to *our* human community, but they have a much stronger claim upon being family members. And this does not remove the ambiguity of their standing but reinforces it. The usual practice of granting even infantile family members full membership in the broader community does not apply. Nevertheless, within the family unit the recognition of their standing is robust, and on no account do we send family members off to be processed and auctioned. And this remains true even though the family itself is the locus of a great deal of violence and harm.

Depending upon the animal in question, we may share our lives with a pet in ways that overlap with the sharing of a life with a child, sibling, parent or spouse, although it is easier to do this with a cat than with various other creatures and it is, perhaps, easiest of all to do this with a dog. (Cats still retain a high degree of independence and self-sufficiency.) What helps to give force to this claim about an overlap, between the way that we relate to them and the way that we relate to each other, is that many of our desires become conditional upon their well-being. This is what happens when we share our lives with others. And so, when we want to have a wonderful summer or a feast at Yule, Christmas or Passover, what we desire is that these things happen with all other family members present, or if not present at least hale and hearty and well cared for by those who also love them. Our own contentment on these and other occasions would be corrupted by their misfortune. And so the prospect of sending a pet off to be slaughtered for a good price, when the market for meat is at a premium, would make no sense. We might as well cut off our own right arm in the hope that it will do some good. In this respect, we may say that the teacher who sent Marcus off to slaughter was teaching the children about where their food comes from, but not teaching them what it is to have a pet, or what it is to *share* a life. The failing here was both moral and educational.

Where we find it difficult to make sense of this idea of sharing our lives, rather than simply living alongside, the concept of pet is placed under strain. If the children or the teachers at the school did not truly share their lives with Marcus, then he was not, in the relevant sense, a pet. And of course, we *do* speak of having pets in other, less interesting senses than the robust and morally significant one in which we speak of animals as companions and dependents. We cannot, for example, share a life with a 'pet' gold-fish in the way that we can do with a medium-sized land animal with whom a far wider range of interactions is possible. And so, when I write here of what it is to relate to an animal as a pet, I am focusing upon a deeper relation of companionship and not one of legal title. Although exactly how deep the relation is when compared to sharing a life with our children remains open to question.

No doubt, there are all sorts of illusions that pet owners or, in a more generous terminology, animal guardians may fall into and these may give us ground for caution about what we may defensibly claim. There may be many delusions to which pet owners are prone: the belief that your pet is uncharacteristically intelligent, that it understands every word you say; that it has something akin to canine or feline extrasensory perception allowing it to know exactly when you are about to arrive home, and so on. A determination to provide public evidence of a pet's cleverness may even lead some animal guardians to teach their pet tricks that have nothing to do with the animal's evolutionary lineage or with their role as a companion. And we may wonder here about the danger of compromising the animal's dignity in this way.[5]

However, the sharing of a life with an animal is not itself a fiction. Instead, we may regard it as partly constitutive of the relation of pet owner to pet. And because that relation is one of sharing, the terminology of 'owner' is apt to mislead. The rival terminology of 'animal guardian' and 'companion animal' is perhaps better at capturing the fact that this is a way of being with another creature rather than simply possessing it. But for the sake of familiarity, except where it may be illuminating to shift terminology, I will stick to the more familiar terms of 'owner' and 'pet'.

The vulnerability of owners to loss is also not a fiction. *She understands every word I say* is not strictly true, but *Life would just not be the same without her* can be. And here it is the loss of the particular animal that is at stake. In the case of Marcus, it would not have quelled the widespread unease if the teacher had promised faithfully to replace the particular animal in question with a new lamb. To share a life with an animal of any sort is to see it as, at least up to a point, irreplaceable. By contrast, what a farmer tries to care about is the herd or (if they are a specialist breeder) the type. Individual beasts are, above all, tokens of the type although the more time that is spent with them the harder this way of seeing becomes. And it is for this reason that it makes sense to speak of how farmers try to see their animals and to leave open the possibility that they may easily slide into ways of seeing and associated forms of attachment that are of a deeper sort. They may begin to respond to particular animals as one-off, unique creatures and this makes slaughter more of a wrench, or *in extremis* unthinkable. The boundary between livestock and animal companion or pet may become blurred.

It has been suggested by Cora Diamond that treating a creature as a pet is simply inconsistent with seeing it as something that one might eat.[6] But this may firm up the distinction between pets and livestock in a way that is not entirely warranted. Diamond thinks that the concept of a person also has this feature. These are concepts of beings who are not to be eaten and not to be eaten even if they die naturally and without suspicious circumstance, and even if they are killed in a road accident. It may sound odd, in the light of what I have said so far, but I do not think that seeing a creature as a pet necessarily does preclude the possibility of their being eaten in this way by their owner, or at the latter's behest. And in saying this, it is not my intention to put pets in danger (the relation to owners is too deep for any danger to emerge). My point is, rather, that the boundary between pets and non-pets can be blurred even in this respect. When we see, and respond to, an animal as a pet what is precluded is treating it intentionally as a resource that may be harvested and eaten in any way whatsoever. But this is not quite the same as Diamond's point.

When a farmer sells his cattle, he looses control over how and why they are consumed. Livestock are a resource whose final end is, in most cases, distant from the point of production. They are, in the final instance, seen as a commodity in a way that pets are not. What precludes pethood is a certain kind of commodification rather than consumption. And here, we may need to remember that children too may be sold when hardship presses to an extent that is beyond endurance. But we do not, except under conditions of unbearable penury or pressing need, sell either our pets or our children. And those who do sell animals on a more casual basis have not bonded with them as pets, or else they do so as a mechanism of improving the animal's circumstances. They do so for what they persuade themselves to be the animal's own good. And this is conspicuously not what takes place with livestock. Their sale is commerce pure and simple (insofar as commerce can be either of these things).

Even so, to gain a little more insight into the case of Marcus, let us consider two scenarios that may help to make some sense of the unsettling idea of hybrid practices, where animals are *partly* treated as pets and where they are also viewed as something to be eaten. The first is a documented case drawn from a famous anthropological study of the Nuer by Evans-Pritchard.[7] The reader discovers that members of this tribe live with and share their lives with their cattle and that the latter are, at least in part, akin to pets. The Nuer allow the slaughter of these animals only and exclusively for ritual consumption. But it turns out (conveniently) that there are many suitable occasions for a ritual. Even so, the animals slaughtered are not just consumed as lunch. Consumption is, at least in theory, a way of honouring the animal and of bonding with it even more closely. It is a way of keeping it within the tribe. It does not involve an end to sharing but a final fusion. That we may question certain of the assumptions involved in this practice or regard them as fictions, need not lead us to deny that animals could sincerely be regarded in this way. Ancient European burial practices, with the mixing of human and animal bones, may suggest that such ways of thinking were once common.

As a second, and less attractive, example I will present a tale about fox hunting. I present it as a piece of hunting lore. It may have happened and it may not have happened and like a great deal that is said about fox hunting the standing of the tale is unclear. Either way, it runs as follows. The horses used in hunting, at least by the affluent core whose sense of their own status is reinforced by participation, are not work-horses of a bulky and robust but graceless sort. They are pampered creatures more akin to pets than working animals, and they conform to various norms of equine beauty. Upon reaching a ripe old age, or after a fall or accident, a horse that has been 'well hunted' but is past its peak was 'traditionally' killed and then fed to the pack. (It is this part of the story that I present as lore rather than description.)[8]

Even if this were to be the case, the consumption would be by hounds rather than by humans, but the material point is that there seems to be no absolute restriction placed upon such consumption and upon its honorific and 'incorporating' or 'bonding' role. It is the kind of thing that *could* happen and we might understand just why it took place even if we happened to disapprove. And it would not obviously involve any radical misunderstanding of what it is to be a unique individual creature or, in simpler terms, a pet. Feeding a horse to the hounds in this way could be linked to a fiction that the animal lived for hunting, a fiction that may make it seem to be for the best that they are humanely killed once their hunting days are over. And again, in this way, as with the consumption of cattle by the Nuer, the animal could in some remote sense, continue to contribute to, and be part of, the world from which it had been removed.

In both cases, whatever one makes of the actual motives involved as opposed to those that might be stated, it is at least intelligible that an animal might be eaten as a way of honouring its contribution to our shared lives. But auctioning off an animal's meat is a different matter that strays more directly into the territory of simple commodification, of treating a fellow being as a thing, as a potential carcass that may be a source of revenue. And this seems to be the only route to consumption that is left open to most of us in North American and Western European cultures. With our elongated food chains and largely non-rural and post-tribal ways of life, we no longer engage in any kind of honorific consumption. A qualification here is that those who try to practice ethical farming may promote nose-to-tail eating and the taking of time over food preparation as a way of doing justice *to* the animal. But even this is not (or is not normally) practised as a way to bring the animal and its consumer into a further sharing of their existence. The background ideas that would make sense of such an extended sharing of existence have, in most instances, gone. And in the absence of such a background what remains is an available kind of eating that is inseparable from commodification of the animal. Such commodification does not fit together with our enriched concept of *pethood*.

The incongruity can be appreciated in the Marcus case. It is also a feature of a better known popular representation of our relation to pets. In a memorable episode of *The Simpsons*, the central character, Homer, acquires a pet lobster, he feeds the lobster only the best food, takes it on walks, attempts to send it to a finishing school for crustaceans and then accidentally kills it off in a nice warm bath. Incongruity, exaggeration and extremes are traditional comic devices that come together when he subsequently eats his pet lobster in comic remembrance, tearful grief and gastronomic delight. No one else must touch it. This is his own personal gastronomic burden, a way of respecting the lobster and ensuring that it will always be a part of him. It is, he informs his family, what the lobster itself would have wanted. Here we may suspect both that his motives are mixed, and that his grasp of what it is for a creature to be a pet is also flawed. Even so, the semblance of honorific consumption makes his motives questionable rather than transparently selfish, and that is good enough for Homer. It may be easy here to focus upon the shallowness of his care for another creature, but what makes the storyline work is (in part) the retention of an idea of sharing a life together with the recurrence of older ideas of honorific consumption and of bonding in a tangible, physical way. Practised by someone else, in a different context, this kind of bonding might indicate a depth of relation and not its absence.

PETS AND NON-PETS

Above, I have made a move that blurs an important part of the boundary between pets and non-pets. This boundary can be blurred in other ways too. The lines between pet and non-pet do not coincide with those between clever animals and dumb brutes. Cats and dogs can be very smart but so too can rats. They are, quite rightly, taken to be cunning, and some people do, for this reason, keep them as pets (in some restricted sense of the term). But these smart animals are also widely regarded in Western Europe and North America as vermin. Pigs too form an interesting comparison class when compared to our intelligent cats and dogs. They are (on a widespread view) just as smart. And, from what we can tell, whales also seem to be incredibly intelligent creatures with an extremely interesting neural structure. Apart from great apes and humans, they are the only creatures that we know of who have spindle cells (neurons associated in humans with empathy and intuition about others). But in spite of our growing appreciation of their neurophysiology, we cannot tell when they are sad or annoyed or content. Whales and humans remain, in certain respects, in a state of mutual incomprehension. Our lives cannot be shared.

What this goes towards is a simple point. Intelligence alone is not enough to make any animal a suitable pet. It does not set up a clear boundary between the pet and the non-pets. The intelligence of an animal must allow it to interact with us in the complex ways that are partly constitutive of sharing our lives and if it does not do so, then the deep relation of pethood cannot be established. This precondition of the relation is also a precondition for relating to animals as livestock. Like livestock, pets are *in every instance* social animals. We have never succeeded in domesticating any creature that was indifferent to group behaviour or unresponsive to communication. Domestication has always depended upon humans being able to take over some aspects of the role of lead animal, the creature who determines when the group should move, where it should go and with what urgency. Domestication of both livestock and pets requires some level of trust and in the relation of pet to its owner (or owners) the trust can be of a deep sort, with each willing to expose themselves to risk for the sake of the other.

Appreciation of this may add to our understanding of the incredulity about the Marcus case, a case of deliberate commodification and, in a sense, the betrayal of a claimed human–pet bond. A similar public reaction might have been expected if, as a proposed educational device, a class was allowed to raise a puppy as a pet before abandoning it outside of a dog rescue centre. Doing so might have taught the children an extremely important lesson about the perils of attachment and commitment. But we do not teach children about harm by harming them (although this was once done). And we do not teach them about betrayal through acts of betrayal. We use literature and allegories, we engage with the tales that they know and we appeal to their imaginations. We do not introduce the life-long burden of a first betrayal, a point of origin to which they may later be tempted to trace all subsequent failures.

LOVE FOR PETS

To speak here of betrayal is to use very strong terminology. There are certain terms, bound up with valuing, that we are uncomfortable about deploying when we refer to non-humans: 'betrayal' is one, 'family' is another and so too is 'love'. The ambiguous position occupied by pets is a source of unease about their application. And so, for example, Peter Singer writes about 'love' in scare quotes to indicate that this familiar way of speaking may be misleading or at least a form of shorthand.[9] And love itself is a concept of a difficult sort. Love can be shallow or deep and it is the prospect of a deep kind of love for a pet that we may find particularly alarming or sentimental or simply inappropriate.

The familiar things that we say about love indicate its special status among the emotions. To see another being as a suitable object of love (in a deep sense) is to see them as unique, valuable in their own right, and valuable in a deep way, a way that may make us bereft at their loss. Love is, or at least can be, an arresting awareness of value.[10]

Rai Gaita has suggested that there is a sense in which it *discloses* value in a way that nothing else can, in a way that all of our talk about respect and dignity and special or unique properties simply misses. 'Sometimes we see that something is precious only in the light of someone's love for it.'[11] This is an attractive view and one that may shed light upon some of our practices, particularly our reluctance to grant that love for a companion animal is love of a genuine and robust (or deep) sort. (And Gaita too shares a qualified version of this reluctance.) After all, if any creature other than a human can be a *suitable* recipient of such love, it may lead us to question a wider range of our actions, particularly when the boundary between pets and non-pets is neither biologically fixed nor particularly secure. The idea that love for some animal involves nothing more profound than a projection of value, or a transference of reasonable feelings onto an unsuitable object, may be more tempting. Yet, we do use the language of 'love' to make sense of such relations. However, someone might *love* their dog in the second-rate sense that they love basketball rather than the genuine way that they love their daughter. And those who know enough about the limits of their pet's intelligence may be hard pressed to defend the appropriateness of saying that they genuinely love their dog in a deep way, or that it really *is* a member of the family.

One consideration that may incline us towards a sceptical view either about the fact of love or about its appropriateness is the ease with which affection and care are given and received. Drawing from her experience as a counsellor, Liz Margolies notes that 'Pets are devoted, forgiving, affectionate, uncritical and available. Their love is given unconditionally.'[12] Those who find their relations with other humans are strained, or repeatedly unsuccessful, may find the companionship of a pet to be a great consolation. Whatever we make of the claimed unconditionality of their love, cats and dogs do not ask us awkward questions, although they may prompt us to ask questions of ourselves. Relationships with other humans are more fraught, prone to a different and life-corrupting set of misunderstandings and uncertainties. Compared to some of the familiar misunderstandings between one human for another, the fantasy that one's animal companion understands every word she is told may be a misunderstanding of a lasting and innocuous sort. This ease and accessibility of affection with pets, compared to its difficulty in the case of humans, may incline us to hold that it lacks depth, that it is all surface, although as a concession it may then be thought of as training for the real thing. Children are, after all, given pets and (with some supervision and overview) allowed to look after them in the hope that they will learn something about caring for another creature. They can come to love a cat or a dog at an age when we would not take seriously their claim to be in love with a classmate, at an age when the only claims of love that we are inclined to accept are the child's claims to love family members, and at an age when they are not yet embarrassed to make such claims.

And adult pet owners too may say that their pets are *like* their children but they would not save the life of a pet in preference to a child unless they were grossly idiosyncratic or psychologically disturbed. Rai Gaita is sensitive to the point and uses it to claim that humans are precious to us in a way that no other creature can be:

> I know of no one whose dog would be treated as equal to a seriously sick infant. If someone did treat their dog like that I would not think of them as a pioneer of ethical thought, but as someone whose sentimentality had made them wicked.[13]

The contrast is well made, but it is not clear exactly how much work it can be made to do. Colin Blakemore wants to use it to suggest that ultimately humans do matter in ways that other animals do not, and that the contrast supports a practice of serious-minded experimentation upon animals.[14] But this over-simplifies. Many people would not save the life of an ageing parent in preference to saving the life of their child, and this is not because of any lack of genuine and deep love (and it is certainly not because elderly relatives are a good candidate for the enquiring scalpel). It is, rather, because children have a priority claim upon us, a claim that we take to trump other serious considerations.

This need not imply the absence of love of other and deep sorts. It simply implies that the *bond* of parent and child, and the moral dimensions of it, can run deep in a special and unique way. However, we love a pet, and whatever the genuineness and depth of talk about our love for pets, we do not love them in quite the same way that we love our children. Our love for pets is love of a different sort. But it is not necessarily of a shallow sort that would preclude our risking of our own life to save a pet even while we would not risk the life of a son or a daughter in order to do so. Every year there is a death toll of adult humans who have tried to rescue their own pets or those of others from fast running rivers. We know this, we know the dangers and we may know that dogs usually make it exhausted to the river bank on their own. But people still wade in, owners and strangers too, who have no special bond with the distressed and drowning animals but who see them as creatures who can be loved and cherished, creatures with whom a life truly could be shared.

Even so, the comparison with children jars. Insofar as our con-cern for a pet and for a child is different, the language of love and of family membership may seem to be used in the absence of a more suitable and accurate terminology. Consideration of a parallel scenario may help to illuminate the point. In the 1970s, television dramatization of Alex Haley's *Roots*, an account of one man's quest to trace his slave ancestors back to Africa, a character known as Chicken George occupies a position that is, for a slave, one of privilege. He trains fighting cocks for his sporting master and travels with him to the fights. At a suitably ill-timed moment, he claims that the master is *like a father* to him. This is shortly before the master bursts in through the door with a shotgun and threatens everyone present in a disturbingly unpaternal way. This is not so-called 'tough love', it is not love at all.

This scenario is a work of fiction but not of fantasy. Such a circumstance could have occurred. The master's imagined behaviour would not have been aberrant or unusual for someone faced with slaves as property, as responsibility and as nearby threat. In the story, a member of his real family had found a small piece of glass in their food, the result of accident or intention. Ambiguity helps the story to work but the author and audience would both have known that a slave in the ante-bellum South could have been spoken of as part of the family but could not have *been* part of the family in the deep sense that would pose a dilemma for his master when faced with a choice between caring for them and protection of kith and kin.

The additional consideration that our relation to our pets is, in some respects, also one of abiding dominance may tempt us to extend this comparison further and to treat the fictional family membership of slaves as a suitable analogy for the way that pets are integral to our lives. Both pets and slaves are, after all, subject to dominance of various sorts, although it may be a mistake to say, as Yi-Fu Tuan, does that the addition of affection to dominance marks the main difference between the two. After all, affection need not be absent from a slave system. Besides which, there are some obvious differences in economic role.[15] Even house-slaves (as opposed to field hands) are a resource and investment in a way that pets are not. In this respect, there is a closer connection between slaves and livestock than there is between slaves and pets. Pets, like children, have always been, conspicuously, a drain upon resources, a drain for which there is usually no material return.

However, it is not obvious that expenditure without return (other than affection) must necessarily be an expression of love. A good deal of commercial activity is habitual (like shopping). The well-being of an end beneficiary (human or animal) can be incidental. It is, more particularly, the capacity for grief rather than the presence of a market for pet products that gives support to the idea that a life with a companion animal may be a life that is genuinely shared and is not a life of one-sided emotional engagement. Grief for the loss of a companion animal, rather than commercial activity on their behalf, may disclose the depth of love in a way that nothing else does. Reports of the symptoms of grief upon the loss of a companion animal do not differ greatly from what we would expect in the case of grief at the loss of humans: anger, guilt, despair combined with a reported loss of sleep, loss of appetite, longing and withdrawal. Duration can also be drawn out, with one estimate suggesting that the state of listlessness usually lasts somewhere between 6 months and a year and with the acute phase lasting for somewhere between 2 and 6 months.[16]

Less clinically, we may refer to the personal experience of being with a pet during its final weeks and days. In a biographical work, *The Dogs who Came to Stay*, the philosopher George Pitcher describes how the arrival of a stray dog allowed him to work through feelings of grief that had long remained bottled up. Raised in a family where open shows of emotion were frowned upon, the openness of the dog's care for its young, and his own growing feelings for the dog were a valuable personal education. The stray dog, later named Lupa, 'taught me how to be with a person in her dying, how to comfort her . . . how to say farewell. And taught me, at last, how to grieve'.[17] But here we may notice something suspect. In many instances of concern for pets, at least as it is reported by adults, the concern takes place against the background of a troubled history. And this may lead us to suspect that a kind of displacement is at work, that the grief while genuine and not in any way 'faked up', is *about* some or other human.

Liz Margolies provides an interesting case of care for a companion animal that might support this picture. A woman whose mother had died leaving her to look after a dog would, at considerable inconvenience, go home from work every single lunchtime in order to check on the dog and to make sure that it was fine. She would be distressed and alarmed if the dog did not greet her immediately upon her arrival home.[18] Here we may see that care for humans can become displaced into care for a pet. And the death of such a pet may be an opportunity for grief that might not otherwise find an effective outlet.

This is not at all unusual. I would go as far as to suggest that it is a normal feature of grief that it is *about* more than the particular death with which we are directly confronted. But this does not obviously mark any difference between our emotional responses to animals and our emotional responses to humans. Neither are pure reactions to an immediately present circumstance. (In slightly more technical terms, emotions have *mixed* intentionality.) Grief, whether it is for a companion animal or for another human, is also about the deaths that have gone before and it can also involve recognition of our own mortality, of the unavoidable and disturbing fact that we shall one day die and may be grieved for in turn. In this respect, grief for a fellow creature who does not belong to our own species, may involve a deep recognition of our own humanity but may still be no less a genuine case of grief for the creature in question.

Granted that the love owners claim to have for their pets may be of a real and deep sort, it can still be suggested that it is, for this very reason, disproportionate. And here we might think of those newspaper stories (apocryphal and otherwise) in which a self-styled 'animal lover' bequeaths her considerable fortune to a favourite cat. And this may seem not only disproportionate but also vaguely misanthropic. It is, after all, anyone's guess just how many people are now homeless, destitute and without hope. We may compare this with our *growing* budget for pet care, for pet treats, for pets themselves, as well as for pet charities and pet hospitals. And, of course, we *can* be disproportionately concerned about the other creatures with whom we share our lives just as we can be disproportionately concerned about a human with whom we do so. But the idea that deep and genuine love for pets must automatically be disproportionate or misplaced draws from an oversimplification of what moral life is like, a view that makes it difficult to situate personal affection and intimate bonds of any sort, including bonds with other humans. We regularly privilege human family and friends over strangers whose needs are in many instances more pressing. And in many instances we are right to do so.

We would not, for example, admire a parent who neglected her own children in order to work for Oxfam even though she would probably, by making this sacrifice, have a greater and more positive impact upon a much larger number of lives.[19] The parent that we admire is the one who can *balance out* the special claims, wants and needs of his or her family, friends and particular others, against those of strangers without utterly neglecting one or the other. And the ways in which we try to do this are situation-dependent in various respects. A parent might, on some occasion, give a child a birthday or Christmas present that consists of a letter explaining that a certain amount of money has gone to a charitable project to save or improve the lives of distant strangers. And this might be a valuable thing to do in all sorts of ways. But if this were the only kind of present that the child was ever given we would regard such behaviour as reprehensible. It would fail to show the special position that the child occupies in the parent's life and the importance of the bond between them.

Our peculiarly human way of living as a particular kind of social animal involves sensitivity to such bonds and to a variety of calls that they place upon our attention. There are our own interests to consider and those of wife, husband, partner, children (who will in turn have different sorts of wants and needs), pets with whom we may have a long shared history, more distant family members, strangers in the street, strangers on TV and in remote places, and the world in general. It is possible to be excessively or dispropor-tionately preoccupied with any one of these interested parties to the exclusion or unfair detriment of others. But it is not obvious that a balancing out of human interests with the needs of com-panion animals is in any way different from our normal ways of caring. And the latter involve doing justice to our personal ties.

7 Experimentation in Context

CAN MEAT-EATERS OPPOSE EXPERIMENTATION?

Let us suppose that you are a conscientious carnivore and that, at least some of the time you buy ethically reared meat. Let us assume that you have a fondness for pets although you may be unsure about how best to describe it. Let us also assume that you are uneasy about animal experimentation. One evening you find yourself eating with someone who is involved in such experimentation. They may be a fully qualified scientist, a lab assistant or a member of the care staff who look after the animals for most of the time. You express your unease and they look over, check the contents of your plate and smile. You are a meat-eater and so, they explain, you have no basis on which to object to experimentation. It may seem that they have a good point and that the existence of a widespread practice of meat-eating *weighs* heavily and perhaps decisively in favour of tolerating a system of intrusive experimentation. My suggestion will be that it *weighs* against doing so, although it may take a little work to explain why.

Here, it may be rather a legalistic objection to point out that the animals we eat and the animals we experiment upon are usually different types of creature. Less than 5 per cent of lab animals in the United Kingdom are cows, pigs, goats, sheep or deer. The vast majority are rodents, mice mainly, rather than the stereotypical lab rats or guinea pigs.[1] Mice are cheap to breed and successive generations can be monitored over a short time-scale. We may imagine that these relatively small, and to some of us, unpleasant, animals are suitable for experimentation, while others (cats, dogs, cows and goats) are less suitable. And lab staff may even come to think of this division as quasi-natural even though it is the result of social history.[2]

One morally significant difference between at least some instances of meat-eating and at least some instances of experimentation is that the latter can have a non-trivial and laudable purpose: the acquisition of knowledge and, secondarily, the improvement of human life. By comparison, while meat-eaters may believe that there is something deeply important and deeply human about their practice, in most cases this will be a mistaken view. (Or so I have attempted to show in the opening chapter.) At the very least, we may say that meat-eating is not normally required for our well-being. And this may make it seem less defensible than serious-minded experimentation. But in making this observation, an observation which may seem comparatively favourable to experimentation, the attempt to equate the moral content of meat-eating and experimentation is set aside. And this may be the right way to go.

The operational requirements of a carnivorous diet and of experimentation can, after all, be significantly different. The only harm that is indispensable to meat production is the violence of killing, the harm of deliberately inflicting death, together with any pain that this involves. We may not think that this is cruel, but of course it can be, if, for example, a creature is killed before it has had a chance of a decent life, or if the stunning procedures are themselves distressing or painful, or if the stunning fails and the animal is hoisted up by one leg and conveyed in distress through the initial stages of processing. Cruelty itself may be extremely hard to define but it is tempting to say that, like violence, you know it when you see it. And even without pain or distress there is a sense in which the killing of an animal can be cruel, at least by familiar standards of cruelty. The painless killing of a pet and the auctioning off of its meat would be, by obvious standards, a cruel betrayal of trust. But the killing of livestock is not like this. It may be morally problematic but there is no comparably deep human–animal relationship to be betrayed. And to say this is to accept that cruelty is not an essential feature of meat-production, although it is a regular accompaniment of its industrialization and of certain kinds of unmodified and ritualized slaughter that demand that an animal be conscious at a crucial stage in the process.

Because of this, the strongest analogy that may be drawn here is between a routine or normal experimental system and the least-defensible forms of meat production. I refer here to 'normal experimentation' because no appeal need be made to the more outlandish and unusual procedures, which might easily be dispensed with. We do not need to expose primates to radiation in order to figure out that it is debilitating; we do not need to bury live pigs in the snow in order to figure out the likely effects of hypothermia and we do not need to get beagles to smoke cigarettes in order to figure out that it is an active cause of cancer. All of these things have been planned or carried out (a snow burial was recently cancelled in Austria after a public outcry).[3] These actions have no plausible defence. But they are not the current norm and it is the norm that we must consider if we are to identify the typical kinds of harm that experimentation (by which I also mean physically intrusive experimentation) cannot readily do without.

Conveniently, the monthly abstracts of the research for which licenses have been granted in the United Kingdom are published online. The details of exactly what is done to the animals is, admittedly, slight, sometimes to the point of being cryptic, and the justification tends to be the (difficult to establish) claim that living systems yield information that is not available from other sources. The 36 licenses granted in February 2009 included the licensing of the following: tests upon about 3,500 genetically modified mice bred to be susceptible to gastrointestinal cancer or exposed to chemical carcinogens; the replacing of parts of unspecified animals with implant material to test the biocompatibility of implant devices for humans; the inducing of lung disease similar to asthma in around 5,000 mice over the course of 5 years, in order to test the effects of potential new medicines; the study of hyperactivity of airways in around 150 genetically modified mice with cystic fibrosis mutations functioning as an imperfect animal model of cystic fibrosis in humans; the implanting of electrodes into the brains of just under 1,000 genetically modified mice and rats, under anaesthetic, and the subsequent monitoring of their behaviour and analysis of their brain tissue to improve our understanding of brain structures; injection of leukaemia cells taken from human patients into around 2,500 mice with under-active immune systems, with some subsequent irradiation to nurture the cells and allow them to become established and their growth to be monitored.[4]

In each case, the harms involved are not at all like those required for meat production. Quite apart from the bodily harm of death (which is the norm for both lab animals and livestock), these kinds of harm are built into the experimental system. It requires pain, non-fatal bodily harm and privation. While we may imagine that, within a civilized system of experimentation, pain relief would be the norm, 61 per cent of UK procedures in 2007 were carried out without any anaesthetic.[5] This is neither unusual nor a matter of sadistic neglect. Procedures are not always complex or drawn out and the administration of anaesthetic can itself be stressful to creatures who are unused to being handled by humans. Some procedures also cannot be reliably carried out under anaesthetic because it thins the blood and may result in haemorrhaging and/or the distortion of results. (The tattooing of humans is carried out without anaesthetic for similar reasons.) Other procedures cannot be executed under anaesthetic because the experiments in question require the monitoring of behaviour on the part of a living, conscious system, under conditions of physical stress.

But even without either deliberately inflicted pain or physical trauma, there are other harms that are built into the experimental system. Lab animals are shut-off from any possibility of enjoying (even briefly) the kind of life that would be a good life for a creature of their kind. They are bred for purpose, usually by companies that specialize in their production or rather over-production, given that many animals do not make it into the data. They are killed as excess to experimental requirements. As specified above, these purpose-bred animals are also, in many cases, genetically modified in harmful ways to have some afflic-tion or susceptibility. They are then reared in hygienically isolated institutional environments, which, even when marginally enriched by the care staff, remain impoverished and cut-off from the life to which the creatures in question are biologically adapted. Laboratories and accommodation blocs are not grasslands, woods, waterways or forests.

There is a reason for this isolation. To avoid experimental results being skewed, lab animals must be pathogen free, that is free of disease or infection. And guaranteeing this requires an extreme curtailment of the risky things that creatures ordinarily do on a day-to-day basis. Any farmer or ethologist (someone who observes animals in the wild as opposed to the laboratory) knows that they can be almost wilfully determined to put themselves in harm's way. Care in a hygienic environment may be, in all sincerity and without 'spin', equated by experimenters and care staff with good treatment. They may even point out that this allows the animal a life that is free from hunger and predation, both of which are normal features of a life in the wild. But for wild animals the risks of predation and hunger are balanced against a measure of freedom to engage in a wide range of natural behaviours, the chance to breed and to have what is (for whatever kind of animal we consider) a good if short life. Given a choice between life in the wild for some creature and life as a lab animal, it would be peculiar to choose the latter for the sake of the animal itself. Sanitized protective custody may offer certain kinds of institutionalized safety but it involves a severe curtailment of any opportunity for an approximation to natural well-being.

By ordinary standards this kind of treatment would be regarded as cruel. But we hesitate to make this judgement in the context of experimentation because the harms involved are not gratuitous. (At least not in the case of experiments that are well thought-out.) Experimental procedures have a purpose and (in at least some cases) a good intention. They are not cruel in the sense of 'cruel' that is sometimes applied to fox hunting or in the more human-directed sense of 'cruel' that we find spoken of in Freud. (They do not involve sadomasochistic harm.) Experiments may seem necessary if we are to secure some good. But there is a long history (particularly in talk about statecraft and politics) of linking cruelty to the perception of unfortunate necessities, to things that need to be done even at the expense of otherwise intolerable harms.[6] We also make everyday judgements about cruelty towards animals that flow out of an appreciation of what can happen when our needs are allowed to eclipse theirs. We may judge that keeping large animals in confined spaces, at home or in the zoo, is cruel; removing them from their natural habitats for our viewing pleasure is cruel; setting aside their biological needs is cruel; keeping pets alive in a state of suffering is cruel, even if it is done for the sake of a child or an owner who cannot bear to part from the animal. Cruelty in these cases does not require sadism or gratuitously inflicted suffering. It can have a point and a purpose. But again, like violence, unless we are desensitized to it through repeated exposure, as slaughterhouse and lab personnel may be, we know it when we see it.

If we make this judgement, that cruelty genuinely is an inbuilt part of the experimental system, we need not be denying that those who inflict a variety of harms upon animals may inflict them for a reason, and we need not suggest that the harms that they inflict are on a par with taunting and beating, or with the spectacular enjoyment of animal suffering. Those who inflict the harms in question may even have a high opinion of their own fondness for animals, even to the point of overcompensation. (It is not unusual for experimental institutions to carry pictures of happy animals in the wild on their walls, or for experimenters to own pets.) But it is only by arbitrarily restricting the concept of cruelty to exclude a certain class of harms inflicted in the name of science, that experimentation can be regarded as other than cruel. Without such a restriction we may have to accept that the system is cruel because of what is deliberately done to the animals, because of what they are forced to go through and because of the life opportunities that they are comprehensively denied. It is cruel in a way that rearing livestock on open pasture is not cruel, even though the latter is inseparable from harm of a different sort.

To classify matters in this way may provoke the counter-claim that it is cruel to allow humans, in particular children and the vulnerable, to suffer when we can perhaps do something about it. This may be true and it is conceivable that it might be a winning argument in favour of experimentation. It is, after all, a feature of our familiar ways of speaking about cruelty that we do some-times regard omissions as genuine instances. However, at best, this places us in the territory of trading-off one kind of cruelty against another. It does not diminish the cruelty of the way in which lab animals are treated, and it does not remove our obligation to recognize what is done.

WHAT EXPERIMENTATION ASSUMES

In order to justify animal experimentation we would need to make at least two important assumptions. The first and most obvious is that it is a reliable way to benefit humans. We may call this the *Reliability Assumption* and state it as follows:

> **The Reliability Assumption**: experimentation delivers real human benefits

Steve Jones, the professor of genetics at University College London, puts the matter succinctly, 'my own judgement (and that of most biologists) is that, with proper controls, the gain from such experiments outweighs the pain they may inflict.'[7] And this balancing-up of cost against gains makes no sense if the gains are a fiction. The second required assumption is that our vital interests are more important than those of the creatures that we experiment upon (which is pretty much every kind of creature there is, with the exception of some primates). We might call this the *Priority Assumption* and state it in these terms:

The Priority Assumption: non-trivial human interests trump animal interests

This would still not give us an entitlement to experiment for trivial reasons, such as the production of perfume and cosmetics, and legislation against experimentation for the latter is now being rolled-out across Europe. (It is also conceivable that the United States will follow, if only to avoid commercial disadvantage.) It should also be pointed out, in the interests of fairness, that some prominent defenders of scientific experimentation, such as Professor Colin Blakemore, the former Chief Executive of the Medical Research Council and a probably the best-known UK advocate of experimentation, have a track record of opposing experimentation for such trivial purposes.

If there is a plausible justification of the experimental system (however restricted or revised), it will be couched in terms of its benefits to humans. Animals too *can* benefit from experimentation and a minority of experiments are geared towards this end. But the experimental system involves extensive overall harm to animals. According to Home Office figures, 3,125,826 animals were experimented upon in the United Kingdom in 2007, and this is almost exactly the average (mean) figure for UK experimentation since 1945.[8] Over the course of the last 65 years, the United Kingdom has experimented on something approaching 195 million animals. And the United Kingdom is just one of the world's major experimenters. The US data are less clear-cut and the largest group of animals, rodents, tend not to be counted, but by aggregating the available figures for the separate states and by assuming that the ratio of rodents to other animals is broadly similar to that in the United Kingdom, we can arrive at a figure of around 10 million animals experimented upon annually.[9] (I have seen estimates that are much higher but it is not clear what they are based upon.) Experimentation is also extensive in France (the United Kingdom's main European competitor) and the figures for Japan may again be close to the 10 million mark. (Quantification is itself an area of dispute.)[10] If accurate, this puts experimentation in the major free-market economies over the last two to three decades at least around the billion mark. The Nuffield Council on Bioethics puts the global figure higher, at somewhere between 50 and 100 million annually, but points out, in a nice understatement, that 'the total number of animals used annually in research around the world are difficult to obtain.' This is not an area of scientific and commercial activity noted for its transparency.

Even if the global figures are towards (or beyond) the upper range of the estimates, this would still mean that far fewer animals fall victim to experimentation than to the livestock system (the slaughter figures for the United States alone are over 10 billion annually) but it is still enough to make a justification of the experimental system by appeal to animal interests implausible.[11] They are, overall, and by any obvious measure, the victims of the process.

Once it is clearly restricted to benefiting humans, the *Reliability Assumption* has a good deal going for it. There is no convincing case to show that *on the whole* experimentation fails to deliver benefits. There *are* many individual cases where experimentation is pointless, uninformative, badly conceived and downright misleading. And in recent times a well-publicized article in the *British Medical Journal* did point out that the legal requirement for pharmaceutical experimentation was resulting in animal experiments being run in parallel with human trials.[12] And it is also true that there have been disasters, such as the drug Thalidomide in the 1960s, which tested safe on animals but led to deformity in the foetal development of thousand of humans. And there are experimental procedures that never reach publication and others that are primarily about data for journal articles. LD50 tests are perhaps the most notorious: some group of animals is given (or forced to take) an input (of whatever sort) until exactly half of them die giving us a precise, quantifiable figure of the 'Lethal Dose for 50 %'. And LD50 tests often generate calls for other LD50 tests extending the data to different kinds of animals.

It is also true (but not widely known) that most experiments have absolutely no direct applicability to human *well-being* and do not claim to be directly useful. (Only about a fifth of current UK experiments are applied research.)[13] And it is both true that there are significant differences between humans and animals and that the biological sciences would not come grinding to a halt if intrusive experimentation was ended.

Be that as it may, there have also been major successes, such as the isolation of insulin and the development of an oral polio vaccine. Both of which involved animal testing. These are historic cases, from half a century ago, and the procedures used then might not be allowed now, but there is at least some case for saying that experimentation did contribute significantly to the results. More fundamentally, Colin Blakemore is right to point out that the overwhelming weight of opinion in the biological sciences is that current testing does work (not all the time, but overall). Steve Jones has even suggested that a refusal to accept the effectiveness of the experimental system amounts to 'science denial' and that, in this respect, it is comparable to creationism.[14] This may be a rather harsh way of putting matters, given that there simply are no large-scale impact studies. Those who challenge the effectiveness of the system can, after all, be wrong without being wrong in the way that those who deny evolution are wrong. Nonetheless, scientists do seem to be our most appropriate authority on this question and few people are ready to believe that the scientific consensus is wildly wrong. If their overwhelming consensus supports the *Reliability Assumption*, then we have a good reason to accept it, as a matter of trust, which is exactly what most of us do.

To say this may invite a charge of being naïve and too trusting and perhaps we *should* be more sceptical. We can, after all, trust too much. There is even a famous psychological experiment to back up this claim. In the 1970s, an experiment was devised to test the willingness of humans to allow authority to over-ride our normal ways of acting. The Milgram Experiment (repeated many times since) involved groups of test subjects being instructed that they were assisting in a procedure that required electric shocks to be delivered to a man in a separate cubicle. (A nice separation was to be maintained.) They were instructed to give an increasingly high series of shocks while the scientist (in white lab coat, with a clip-board or otherwise with the regular and reassuring paraphernalia) took note of the effect. The situation, as we might expect, was a set-up. We are not allowed to torture or be cruel to humans for scientific purposes. And even with some non-trivial purpose, torture and cruelty would have been involved if the procedure were genuine. The human test-victim was simply mimicking the effects of being horribly shocked (groaning, screaming and so on). At the 300-volt level, which is significantly more than the mains supply in either the United States or the United Kingdom and easy enough to kill someone, he pounded on the walls. At 315 volts, he made no further response. With each indication of reluctance to go on, the experimental subjects were told to continue, that it was necessary to the experiment. In the initial Milgram Experiment, *all* the shock-inflicting test subjects went above the lethal 300-volt level. None of them refused. They differed only in terms of the rationalizations that they offered afterwards. Trusting too much can be a real problem.

Here we have a classic case of an excessive willingness to defer to scientific authority. We may imagine that in similar circumstances, we would show more restraint and character. The experimental results suggest otherwise but they may now be out of date. The experiment is now difficult to reproduce because it is so well-known and people catch on to what is happening. In earlier days, only a small minority of individuals proved resistant. But here, I want to suggest that the problem in both the Milgram case and in the case of animal experimentation is not simply one of deferring to scientific authority, but of deferring to such authority on moral matters as well as scientific ones. Controversial experimental procedures combine both. Observing the impact of electric shocks could indeed provide useful scientific information. On this matter, a scientist would be the appropriate authority. But the ethics of inflicting harm of this sort, in order to gain knowledge, is a matter on which scientists have no special standing. On questions of this sort they are no more authoritative than you or I.

What this means is that scientific reassurances should be accepted only in the case of the *Reliability Assumption* and not in the case of the *Priority Assumption*. Scientists may occupy some position within a set of structures that are geared to systematically favour human interests over animal interests but the assumption that it is right to do so requires some further justification. Colin Blakemore attempts to provide such justification in familiar terms by appeal to a trade-off situation in which we can only save humans or animals.

> I'm very fond of animals, I have kept pets all my life, but if it came to a choice between my cat, which has lived with us for some 7 years and is very much a part of the family, and the life of one of my daughters, I would not have the slightest hesitation in saying the life of my daughter should have priority; and I think that most people would feel the same way. They might love animals, but they see that human beings are just different.[15]

This defence of human priority is an interesting combination of two quite separate points. The first is that humans intrinsically matter more, that they are 'just different' and by virtue of this difference, they are more important than other animals. The second is a claim about bonding. And bonding is something that I have already suggested is morally significant.[16] Blakemore's appeal to his own daughter serves as a useful model for our relation to all humans: we have a special connection to humans that we do not have to other creatures. A noteworthy feature of this claim about bonding is that it does not depend upon any appeal to our humanity making us more valuable than non-humans.

THE ARGUMENT FROM MARGINAL CASES

Let us consider the claim that humans are just different and by virtue of this difference, more important than other animals. One way to make sense of this is by appeal to various properties or competences that we have: our capacity for abstract thought, for language use, for certain kinds of reasoning, self-consciousness, and also for special kinds of suffering and enjoyment. The problem is that we do not *all* have these properties. Some humans are cognitively impaired in quite radical ways. The extreme case would be a human in a coma. Others do not yet have the relevant properties because they are infants. But at least in the case of developmentally normal human infants, there is some potential to acquire the admired and valued properties at some later stage. So let us focus only upon those humans who lack such potential, who have irretrievably lost these properties or whose genetically fixed makeup renders them incapable of ever acquiring the properties in question. Would we tolerate experimentation upon such unfortunates? Probably not, although it has been done in the past. Currently, as a matter of law, we would not be allowed to. But if we hold that experimentation upon such humans is wrong, then presumably, as a matter of consistency, we should also hold that it is *just as wrong* to experiment

upon other creatures with similar or greater cognitive competences and a similar or greater capacity for suffering.

Perhaps we might think of this as a matter of rights. We might
then emphasize the kind of consideration that appeals to one
sort of philosopher (Tom Regan) rather than others (such as Peter
Singer) who prefer to focus upon capacity for suffering. But we
need not take sides here. The key point of this argument, known
to philosophers as the *argument from marginal cases*, is that
there seems to be no morally relevant property that all humans
have and that all animals lack. (Or, to add a little refinement to the
position, there is no property that humans all have to a greater
degree than all non-humans.) As a result, it seems that we have no
solid basis for drawing a hard and fast distinction between what
can be done to *us* and what can be done to *them*. As a matter of
avoiding prejudice, it seems that humans and cognitively comparable non-humans should be accorded the same standing,
whatever that standing turns out to be. If there are constraints
upon what we can do to one, there are similar constraints upon
what we can do to the other. A refusal to accept this may leave us
open to a charge of 'speciesism' by analogy with 'racism' and to
a lesser extent 'sexism'.

This argument may seem so counter-intuitive in its implications
that it simply must be wrong for reasons that are not, at present,
clear. If we accept its implications, then perhaps we would gain a
certain kind of consistency in our outlook, but it is not obvious
that consistency takes priority over all other considerations. It is
not obvious that we should abandon intuitions at the first sign
of tensions in our beliefs and attitudes. Perhaps there are times
when we should stick by our deepest intuitions and not be overly
impressed by arguments that take aim at deep moral commit-
ments. And one of these is our commitment to the importance
of humanity.

But, in fairness to what has become known as the *argument
from marginal cases*, it does not conflict as greatly with our
ordinary intuitions as we might initially expect. Most normal

humans do turn out to have life opportunities that most non-humans lack. And developmentally normal humans do usually have a capacity for suffering that is greater than most non-humans. We have an appreciation of time that opens up possibilities for guilt, remorse, regret and anxiety, and these are present only in an attenuated form in other animals. Even if we accept the *argument from marginal cases*, considerations of this sort would still impact upon the life and death decisions that we would be able to justify. So, for example, if we had to decide between saving the life of a cognitively normal human (with reasonable life expectations) or saving the life of a cognitively normal mammal of some other sort, then we ought to save the former. With Peter Singer, we might say that both creatures would have an interest in continuing to live, but the human would probably have a greater interest in doing so. Alternatively, we might say with Tom Regan that the *creatures* would be of equal value but the *lives* on offer would not. A decision in favour of the human might then reasonably be taken on such a basis without any suggestion of species prejudice.

Nonetheless, in the rare or exceptional cases where a non-human turned out to have the better life opportunity, or the greater interest in continuing to live, this approach would lead us to save the non-human. Being human would not be enough to warrant better treatment than non-humans. That is to say, the *Priority Assumption* would have to be abandoned.

THE IMPORTANCE OF CONCERN FOR HUMANS

One way to avoid this would be to say that humanity itself is a morally relevant property that every single human has (even coma victims) and that every other animal lacks. If this position could in some way escape the charge of being a mere prejudice, then it might provide some reason for prioritizing non-trivial human interests over the interests of other animals and might, in doing so, provide some justification for a system of experimentation. Blakemore appeals to something of this sort as his second line of defence for experimentation. He points out that we have a special *bond* with other humans, a bond that is in some respects comparable to the family bond and that does not require any dubious assumptions about humans being more *valuable* than non-humans irrespective of the properties that they happen to possess.

Appeal to this kind of bond is consistent with accepting that all animals may, in some sense, be equally valuable but there are nonetheless some grounds for favouring one group of creatures over another. Similarly, let us suppose that you have a daughter. She will be valuable beyond price but no more so than anybody else's daughter. Yet, if forced to decide, you would clearly have reasons to save her life at the expense of the daughter of a stranger, relative or neighbour. Similarly, your dog is no more intrinsically valuable than any other dog, but you still have reasons to care for and cherish it that you do not have to care for and cherish other dogs. What matters in each case is the bond that exists between humans who live together and care for each other, and sometimes, between humans and the animals with whom they regularly interact and who form part of their families.

Blakemore alludes to the bond shared between humans in family terms, but we do not, of course, have any personal and intimate connection to all humans, so the analogy with family ties is of a fairly loose sort. But if we do not have an intimate and personal connection just what sort of connection can there be? An obvious answer here, and the option that Blakemore favours, takes the form of an appeal to biology and to species membership. 'I think it is very important to hang onto one strong moral principle, which is that there is a clear distinction between responsibilities to our own species and our responsibilities to other species.' Similarly, 'we have a responsibility to all species to minimize suffering, but on top of this we have a primary obligation to our own species. This is a very normal biological principal. You see it in virtually every species.'[17]

But here, Blakemore speaks as a scientist who has (albeit in the past) worked in a laboratory, rather than as someone who has observed animals in the wild. In the wild, social animals bond together in local groups and not by any larger grouping. Territorial animals (of which there are many) are hostile to interlopers of the same species, but they tolerate animals of other species with whom they have no particular rivalry.[18] Darwin would seem to be a reasonably good authority on this matter. 'Animals endowed with the social instincts take pleasure in one another's company, warn one another of danger, defend and aid one another in many ways. These instincts do not extend to all the individuals of the species, but only to those of the same community.'[19] And our human past shows this same pattern of local rather than universal attachment. Attachment is as much a social phenomenon as it is a biological one. In line with this, talk about our humanity does not, after all, have the same sense as talk about our species, about *Homo sapiens*. 'Humanity' in this sense is not a biological concept belonging to the natural sciences, but a value concept that belongs to moral discourse. It is a product of history and shares certain features with other non-biological concepts such as 'pet', 'livestock' and 'lab animal'.

Accepting this is not the same as claiming that a shared humanity is a myth or a 'mere' construct. But it does push us towards a particular understanding of what our connection to one another involves. We may think of the bond as, in some respects, comparable to that of belonging to a shared community. Although here, community is in some respects still only a metaphor. Our shared human community is not geographically restricted in the way that communities usually are. In fact, it is extensive enough for us not to know any but a small proportion of the other community members on a personal basis. Nonetheless, the usual minimal conditions for the existence of a genuine community may still apply. That is, we must have a shared history, some shared interests, a capacity on the part of at least some of our number for mutual awareness and for the acceptance of norms that have emerged out of our shared history. Norms of this sort might take the form of taboos or of prescribed and proscribed actions. But without shared norms of some sort there is no genuinely shared life. To appeal to anything analogous to community is, in this way, to make an appeal to certain kinds of shared values. In other respects, these conditions are minimal enough to allow that we may be members of more than one community. We are, for example, creatures as well as humans and may do well to recognize other animals as *fellow creatures* in a sense that involves more that acceptance of a certain biological relation reaching into the distant past.

Our belief that the shared human bond is deep stems in part from an awareness of what has happened in the past when humanity has been overlooked or when it has seemed to be stripped away as it was through slavery, antisemitism and the Holocaust. It is in this loss of recognition, in the failure to acknowledge that others are fully human, that we can see that the human bond is no fiction. What the slave owner denied was the slave's humanity, what the ideologically committed Nazi denied was the humanity of the camp inmates. They were instead vermin or subhuman, just as they appeared to be in the propaganda newsreels. These worrying precedents of racism and of antisemitism, and more generally of prominent instances of extreme prejudice, may give some persuasive force to the idea that our relations with, and ideas about, other creatures might reduce to a comparable prejudice. But these same precedents also give persuasive force to the idea that humanity matters, and that not every kind of concern for fellow humans, simply because they are fellow humans, need be thought of as blind prejudice.

CRUELTY AND MORAL AUTHORITY

To make sense of how we can give humanity its due without lapsing into prejudice let us consider two scenarios, both drawn

from novels by C. S. Lewis.[20] In the first scenario, you have landed
on a nearby planet that is inhabited by three different kinds of
intelligent life form. They are just as clever as humans, although
their lifestyle and desires are somewhat different. You, a human,
now add to the mix. Would your humanity entitle you to any general claim of dominance or priority over these other creatures?
Not obviously. And this would not simply be because you would
be on their planet, or, more simply, dwelling in their territory.
They, in turn, in spite of the territorial advantage, would have no
obvious and general claim of dominance or priority over you.
As equally rational and equally feeling animals you and these
remarkable creatures would all be entitled to a certain kind of
equivalent consideration, although there might be particular
and exceptional contexts in which you would be excluded (e.g.
from particular rituals or from particular traditionally structured
activities).

Even if some of the creatures were to travel back with you to
the Earth, there would still be a straightforward case for saying
that they should again be entitled to equal treatment, perhaps
with some similar specified exceptions. They might not be taken
seriously in beauty competitions or as candidates for certain acting roles. But otherwise, equality would be the norm. In such a
comparison your humanity would seem to make little difference.
What would be important would be the similar competences
that you and these other remarkable creatures happened to
share. Consideration of this first scenario might even lead us to
think that humanity itself is an insignificant consideration when
compared to the possession of various important properties
that might be instantiated in other and quite different non-
human ways.

Now consider a second scenario, one which may suggest that
humanity matters in its own right. This time you find yourself
in the midst of a community of humans who engage in experimentation upon animals and they are rather less constrained in
their actions than our existing experimenters. They feel entitled to

do whatever they wish in order to further their knowledge and to attain a certain state of mind and of being. In this context, a thoroughgoing defence of the unfortunate animals might well depend upon the claim that, in some sense, the experimenters are *betraying* their humanity. And consideration of this second scenario might lead us to think that humanity can matter a good deal, but not in any way that licenses the *Priority Assumption* or any general claim of priority over non-humans.

In the above fictional examples, you the human are in a position to inflict harm and, more particularly, cruelty. Together with other humans you are assumed to be in a position of power. And thinking about *your* humanity and *our* humanity in this context is rather different from thinking about it in the more disturbing and non-fictional examples of the Holocaust and of slavery. It may suggest that our appreciation of humanity does not reduce to identifying with other humans as potential victims. It may also involve preserving our humanity when we are in the ascendant, when we have power over others. There is, after all, a familiar sense in which humanity can be not exactly 'lost' but rather 'betrayed' through actions of any sort that are cruel or, in familiar terms, inhumane.[21] In this respect, it may be worth noting that even the Nazis did not cease to be humans, they did not lose their humanity, but they did betray it. And betrayal of the relevant sort is part of what makes us think of the Holocaust not only as horrific, but also as tragic in a special way.

Even so, it may make sense to hold that humanity can be compromised or betrayed in ways that lack the utter dreadfulness of the Holocaust and betrayed not just in the defence or promotion of dreadful powers. It may be betrayed in the lengths to which we can be driven to promote otherwise worthwhile ideals. George Orwell is perhaps our best authority on this matter. His classic novel *1984* examines the revolt of the last man, Winston Smith, on the brink of losing his humanity to a totalitarian system. But without his help the system cannot take it away. It is Smith who betrays it, by embracing the need for acts of desperate cruelty.

He is ready to do whatever is necessary to bring down Big Brother. Orwell understood that a failure to recognize and to live in line with an appreciation that our humanity may be harmed in this way is not the prerogative only of the malevolent. In our own times, the torturing of captives to secure life-saving information may be a good candidate for a similar act of betrayal. As a more general point, it is cruelty rather than any other kind of moral failing that places us in a special kind of danger.

This is an attractive and controversial line of thought and one that deserves a more detailed elaboration than I have given here. It may also be a line of thought that defenders of experimentation might be keen to resist because they have some inkling of where it is liable to end up. In its favour, it may be pointed out that it allows us to accept the importance of our humanity and to address the problem of marginal cases in an intuitively plausible way. Given a choice between saving the life of a cognitively impaired human and the life of a cat with comparable cognitive competences, we would have an obvious reason to save the human. (Just so long as their life was still worth living.) The human is already the victim of a misfortune of a dreadful sort, one that prevents her full enjoyment of being part of the human community. To pile a further misfortune on top of this, when we can avoid doing so, would be cruel indeed.

But this justification for saving the fellow human in such a case depends upon an appeal to their special and unfortunate circumstances. And in particular it does not require or entail acceptance of the claim that human interests ought to be given *priority* over the interests of non-humans. It does not require us to endorse anything that would license systematically favouring human interests by experimenting upon animals. The hope of those who, like Colin Blakemore, defend experimentation is that an appeal to the human bond (however construed) will work in just this way. But my point is that it need not do so. It depends upon how we make sense of this bond and of what is morally required if we are to embrace and live in line with our humanity.

If, for example, we accept the importance of preserving our humanity by regarding cruelty in a special light, and as a unique kind of threat, then the importance of our shared humanity can be seen to weigh against *any* experimental system that requires cruelty. It may only be one consideration among many when trying to evaluate the merits of experimentation, but it will weigh against the idea that we have any special entitlement to be cruel.

When we take seriously the metaphor of the human community, and to a lesser extent the analogy of the human family, these will not support any open-ended license to favour human interests irrespective of the cost to non-humans. We would not, for example, think well of someone if they channelled their energies only towards the well-being of their own family or of their own community while surrounded on all sides with extreme suffering and harm to strangers. Caring only about our own can be just as flawed as caring only about strangers in need. The person we admire is the one who maintains a reasonable balance between care for their own group and justice towards others.

Moreover, like any other shared bond, our humanity can be a source of reasons for care, for hope and for pride, but it can also be a source of reasons for shame and guilt about the actions of those to whom we are connected. Group identification of whatever sort comes with advantages for social animals. But it also comes at a price. If we are to allow that our group identity as humans is a source of justifications, it will be difficult to see exactly why we should refuse to accept the obligations that also normally result from sharing a bond with others. We may, for example, feel pride in our fellow countrymen for their hospitality towards visitors, their capacity to welcome the stranger in our midst. But if we hear of tourists being robbed or mistreated, we have reasons for something more akin to shame, even though we personally have done nothing wrong. More ominously, it is a terrible thing to find out that a member of one's family, a parent or grandparent, was involved in some massacre, that they colluded in or helped to organize genocide or that one's community or country built its wealth upon slavery.

Carried over to the case of caring for humans and for non-human animals, the fact that animals have historically been mistreated, abused and harmed by *us*, that is by members of our shared human community, gives us a reason to redress the balance. And we are not currently doing so. Industrial meat production is growing, slaughter is growing, and if the UK figures are reliable, so too is experimentation as it races to keep pace with an aging and increasingly medicated population. At the time of writing, in spite of a notional commitment to reduce as well as refine and replace animal experimentation, the scale of experimentation has been steadily rising for more than a decade (since 1997 if a precise turning point is to be identified).[22] What makes this all the more forceful a consideration is that we probably *have* benefited from the proceeds of a strong imbalance in the pattern of care. Our lives may be longer or better or both as a result of a marginalizing and even a trivializing of non-human interests.

To say this is not to present a timeless critique of intrusive experimentation or even a comprehensive one. I would like to see an immediate end to the system but offer only a reason for its curtailment. And I leave open the possibility that somewhere, sometime, experimentation that was not part of some industrially driven routinized system could be justified. After all, if we are prepared to raises the stakes to fictional proportions and to envisage a situation where we must experiment on a single creature, in non-painful but perhaps cruel ways, or else every living thing dies, then we can always envisage circumstances where experimentation would not only be the right thing to do, but would obviously be the right thing to do, even at the expense of cruelty. And I am certainly not appealing to the sacredness of animal bodies. All creatures (humans included) live and die and are part of a reality that exceeds us and that is, in obvious respects, more important than any one of us. And this may make a blanket rejection of experimentation implausible. Tragic circumstances could force ordinary decent moral agents to trade-off certain kinds of cruelty against the imminent prospect of intolerable harm to both humans and other animals.

My point, rather, is that we *as humans* who face no such fictionally extreme scenario, we could only begin to mount a plausible defence of our existing system of extensive and routine experimentation if the remainder of our relations to non-humans were of a more mutually advantageous sort. We could only begin to do so if we had not already placed great burdens upon our fellow creatures. And this returns me to the opening point of this concluding chapter. Defenders of experimentation who want us to think about it in the light of our existing practice of meat-eating are right to do so. However, this connection does not help the case for experimentation. We already harm so why not harm some more is not an appealing line of defence. As a matter of justice or more simply of balance, the existence of a vast and unnecessarily cruel food system weighs *against* any claim that we currently have the moral authority to inflict *further* cruelty and harm. If we ever had such authority, we have long since lost it.

Notes

Chapter 1

1. Peter Singer, *Animal Liberation*, 2nd edition (London: Pimlico, 1995), p.x.
2. Stephen Law, *The Philosophy Files* (London: Dolphin, 2002), p.27.
3. Stephen Law, *The Philosopher's Gym* (London: St Martin's Press, 2003), p.240.
4. For a good critique of 'internalism', see Russ Shafer-Landau, *Moral Realism: A Defence* (Oxford: Oxford University Press, 2003) chapter 6.
5. Elizabeth Telfer, *Food for Thought* (London and New York: Routledge, 1996), p.112.
6. Singer (1995), p.xiv.
7. Cora Diamond, 'Eating Meat and Eating People', in Cora Diamond, *The Realistic Spirit* (Cambridge Mass: MIT Press, 1991), 326 ff.
8. Tanya Barnard and Sarah Kramer, *How It All Vegan* (London: Grub Street, 2008), p.11.
9. *Why Vegan?* (Birmingham: The Vegan Society, no date), p.2.
10. The figure of 10 billion animals slaughtered per annum in the United States comes from Erik Marcus, *Meat Market* (Boston: Brio, 2005), p.5. It is based upon an aggregation of figures published by the USDA (United States Department of Agriculture).
11. For the homepage of the Slow Food Movement, go to http://www.slowfood.com/.
12. Michael Pollan, *The Omnivore's Dilemma* (New York: Penguin, 2006), p.313.

13. Pollan (2006), p.314.

14. Peter Singer and Jim Mason, *Eating: What We Eat and Why It Matters* (London: Arrow, 2006), p.242, see especially pp.245–50.

15. Hugh Fearnley-Whittingstall, *The River Cottage Meat Book* (London: Hodder & Stoughton, 2004), chapter 1 is a very good statement of some of the ethical problems facing meat-eaters and vegetarians.

16. The classic treatment of the linkage between food and embracing life in the late medieval period is Mickhail Bakhtin's *Rabelaise and His World* (Bloomington: Indiana University Press, 1993). However, even Bakhtin's genius need not persuade us to buy into the clear-cut way that he separates out the official renunciatory culture and the popular life-embracing culture.

17. J. M.Coetzee, *Elizabeth Costello* (London: Vintage, 2004), pp.88–9.

18. Barnard and Kramer (2008), p.12.

19. Kosher restrictions are based upon Leviticus 11:1–4 and Deuteronomy, 14: 3–7. The most widely read short account of such restrictions is the classic anthropological treatment of pollution and taboo, Mary Douglas, *Purity and Danger* (London and New York, 2002), chapter 3.

20. V. Messina and A. Mangels, 'Considerations in Planning Vegan Diets: Children', *Journal of the American Dietetic Association*, 101 (2001), pp.661–69; O'Connell et al. 'Growth of Vegetarian Children: The Farm Study', *Paediatrics*, 84 (1989), pp.475–81; T. A. B. Sanders and S. Reddy, 'Vegetarian Diets and Children', *American Journal of Clinical Nutrition*, 59 (1994), pp.1176S–1181S; C. W. Thane and C. J. Bates, 'Dietary Intake and Nutrient Status of Vegetarian Pre-school Children from a British National Survey', *Journal of Human Nutrition and Dietetics*, 13.6 (2000), pp.149–62.

Chapter 2

1. Quoted in Karen Warren, 'The Power and Promise of Ecological Feminism', *Environmental Ethics*, 12.2 (1990), p.146.

2. Bernard Rollin, 'The Ethics of Agriculture: The End of True Husbandry', in Marian Stamp Dawkins and Roland Bonney, *The Future of Animal Farming* (Oxford: Blackwell, 2008), p.7.

3. John Rawls, *A Theory of Justice* (Cambridge: Harvard University Press, 1971), p.512. For a more recent attempt to extend contract theory to cover human-animal relations, see Andrew I. Cohen, 'Contractarianism. Other-regarding Attitudes, and the Moral Standing of Nonhuman Animals', *Journal of Applied Philosophy*, 24.2 (2007), pp.188–201.

4. Douglas (2002), p.xv.

5. Catherine Larrère and Raphaël Larrère, 'Animal Rearing as a Contract', *Journal of Agricultural and Animal Ethics*, 12 (2000), p.55 draws attention to a relevant passage in Lucretius *De Rerum Natura*, although the translation has to be favourable for this reading to be sustained.

6. Stephen Budiansky, *The Covenant of the Wild* (London: Phoenix, 1997), p.24.

7. Budiansky (1997), p.41.

8. Telfer (1996), p.79.

9. Fearnley-Whittingstall (2004), p.23.

10. Leslie Stephen, *Social Rights and Duties* (London: Swan Sonnenshein & Co. Ltd.,1896).

11. For a straightforward defence of slaughter by appeal to the *opportunity of life argument,* see the appendix to Temple Grandin's, *Animals Make Us Human* (New York: Houghton-Mifflin Harcourt, 2009).

12. Fearnley-Whittingstall (2004), p.23.

13. Peter Singer and Jim Mason, *Eating: What We Eat and Why It Matters* (London: Arrow, 2006), pp.57–9.

14. Henry Salt, 'The Logic of the Larder', in Tom Regan and Peter Singer, *Animal Rights and Human Obligations* (New Jersey: Prentice-Hall, 1976), p.186.

15. Singer (1995), p.228; Singer and Mason (2006), pp.248–9; Peter Singer, *Practical Ethics*, 2nd edition (New York: Cambridge University Press, 1993), p.xi.

16. Bernard E. Rollin, *The Frankenstein Syndrome: Ethical and Social Issues in the Genetic Engineering of Animals* (New York: Cambridge University Press, 1995), p.179.

17. Derek Parfit, *Reasons and Persons* (Oxford: Oxford University Press, 1984), chapter 16.

Chapter 3

1. Richard Corliss, 'Should We All Be Vegetarians?', *Time* 15 July 2002.
2. For a compilation of statistics on UK vegetarianism, see http://www. vegsoc.org/info/statveg.html.
3. Pollan (2006), pp.321–2.
4. Barbara Kingsolver, *Animal, Vegetable, Miracle* (London: Faber and Faber, 2007), p.10.
5. Marcel Proust, *In Search of Lost Time* (London: Vintage, 2002), pp.144–5.
6. Moses Maimonides, *A Guide for the Perplexed*, 4th edition (New York: E.P. Dutton, 1904), chapter 48.
7. Martha Nussbaum, *Upheavals of Thought* (New York: Cambridge University Press, 2001), pp.200–6.
8. Plutarch, 'On the Eating of Flesh', in his *Moralia* (Cambridge: Harvard University Press, 1957), volume 12.
9. For an examination of this aspect of Porphyry's treatise, *On Abstinance from Animal Food, see* Catherine Osborne, *Dumb Beasts and Dead Philosophers* (Oxford: Oxford University Press, 2007), chapter 9.
10. Messina (2001); Sanders and Reddy (1994).
11. Michael Pollan's *In Defence of Food* (London: Penguin, 2009) stresses this, but is a little too hasty in its account of the debate about lipids, pp.40–50.
12. E. H. Haddad and S. J. Tanzman, 'What do Vegetarians in the United States Eat?' *American Journal of Clinical Nutrition*, 78 (2003), pp.626S–632S.
13. Fearnley-Whittingstall (2004), p.67.
14. The Vegan Society, *Animal Free Shopper*, 8th edition (Birmingham: The Vegan Society, 2008), pp.43–5.
15. Vegan Society (2008), p.393.

Chapter 4

1. Osborne (2007), p.229.
2. I am grateful to Catherine Osborne for this example.
3. Pollan (2006), p.326.

4. For criticism of organic as import-heavy see James Lovelock, *The Revenge of Gaia* (London: Penguin, 2007), p.155.

5. http://www.ukagriculture.com/food/self_sufficiency_and_crops.cfm.

6. *Amber News*, February 2004.

7. http://www.locavores.com/.

8. http://www.slowfood.com/.

9. Singer and Mason (2006), p.145.

10. http://www.calrice.org/e7b_cas_rice_growing_region.htm.

11. http://westernfarmpress.com/rice/california-rice-0910/.

12. Singer and Mason (2006), p.148.

13. Adrien Myers, *Organic Futures: The Case for Organic Farming* (Devon: Green Books, 2005), pp.215–18.

14. http://www.food.gov.uk/gmfoods/gm/gmanimal.

15. For DEFRA research into the use of home grown chicken feed, see http://sciencesearch.defra.gov.uk/Default.aspx?Menu=Menu&Module=More&Location=None&Completed=0&ProjectID=9479.

16. D. Pimentel and M. Pimentel, 'Sustainability of Meat-Based and Plant-Based Diets and the Environment', *American Journal of Clinical Nutrition*, 78 (2003), pp.660S–663S.

17. Corliss (2002).

18. Herring and Bertrand (2002).

19. Marcus (2005), p.256.

20. Tyson Foods (2005) *Tyson Foods Investor Factbook* (Tyson Foods, Inc.), p.4, available at http://media.corporate-ir.net/media_files/irol/65/65476/reports/04_05_factbook.pdf.

21. Henning Steinfeld, Pierre Gerber, Tom Wassenaar, Vincent Castel, Mauricio Rosales and Cees de Haan, *Livestock's Long Shadow* (Rome: FAO, 2006).

22. James Garvey, *The Ethics of Climate Change* (London: Continuum, 2008), chapter 1.

23. Haddad and Tanzman (2003).

24. Gidon Eshel and Pamela Martin, 'Diet, Energy and Global Warming', *Earth Interactions*, 10 (2006), pp.12, 15.

25. http://demeter.net/.

26. http://rodaleinstitute.org/.

27. Julie Guthman, *Agrarian Dreams* (California: University of California Press, 2004), chapter 2.

28. Michael Pollan, 'The Organic-Industrial Complex', *New York Times Magazine*, 13 May 2001. The publication of this article was a major turning point in the public image of organic.

29. Judith Willis, *The Green Food Bible* (London: Eden Project Books, 2008), p.103, uses this case, and the problem of an over-reliance upon imported Mediterranean-style vegetables to stress the ecological limits of vegetarianism.

30. Osborne (2007), p.229.

31. Marcus (2005), p.73.

Chapter 5

1. Osborne (2007), p.229.

2. Pollan (2006), pp.325–6.

3. Colin Tudge, *So Shall we Reap* (London: Penguin, 2003), pp.334–5.

4. Immanuel Kant, *Lectures on Ethics* (Cambridge: Cambridge University Press, 1997), p.240.

5. Kingsolver (2007), pp.222–3.

6. Pollan (2006), pp.326–7.

7. Kingsolver (2007), p.225.

8. Aldo Leopold, *A Sand Country Almanac* (Oxford: Oxford University Press, 1968), p.196.

9. Steven Davis, 'The least Harm Principal May Require that Humans Consume A Diet Containing Large Herbivores, Not a Vegan Diet', *Journal of Agricultural and Environmental Ethics*, 16 (2003), pp.387–94; Gaverick Matheny, 'Least Harm: A Defence of Vegetarianism from Steve Davis' Omnivorous Proposal', *Journal of Agricultural and Environmental Ethics*, 16 (2003), pp.505–11; Singer and Mason, (2006), p.252.

10. The classic source for the impact of pesticides is Rachel Carson's *Silent Spring* (London: Penguin, 2000), especially chapter 8.

11. For the tie-in to forest clearance see Gaverick Matheny and Kai Chan, 'Human Diets and Animal Welfare: The Illogic of the Larder', *Journal of Agricultural and Environmental Ethics*, 18 (2005), pp.579–94.

12. Myers (2005), p.39.

13. www.wateraid.org for details of composting; and briefly, Louisa Pearson, 'As muck would have it', *Scotland on Sunday*, 15 November 2009.

Chapter 6

1. Andy McSmith, 'Marcus the Sheep Falls Victim to Ruthless Primary School Pupils', *The Independent*, 12 September 2009.

2. Roger Scruton, *Animal Rights and Wrongs*, 3rd edition (London: Metro Books, 2000), p.44.

3. Mary Midgley, 'The Mixed Community', in Midgley *Animals and Why They Matter* (Athens: University of Georgia Press, 1983), p.112.

4. Tony Milligan 'Dependent Companions', *Journal of Applied Philosophy*, 26.4 (2009), pp.402–13.

5. Gary Francione, *Animals as Persons: Essays on the Abolition of Animal Exploitation* (New York: Columbia University Press, 2008).

6. Cora Diamond, 'Eating Meat and Eating People', in Diamond (1991).

7. E. E. Evans-Pritchard, *The Nuer: A Description of the Modes of Livelihood and Political Institution of a Nilotic People* (Oxford: Oxford University Press, 1940), p.27ff.

8. *Flambards*, a 1970s TV soap opera in the United Kingdom, set around a fox hunting family, presents just such a scenario.

9. Singer (1995), p.x.

10. J. David Velleman, 'Love as a Moral Emotion', *Ethics*, 109 (1999), pp.338–74.

11. Raimond Gaita, *Good and Evil: An Absolute Conception* (London: Routledge, 2004), p.xxiv.

12. Liz Margolies, 'The Long Good-Bye: Women, Companion Animals, and Maternal Loss', *Clinical Social Work Journal*, 27.3 (1999), p.298.

13. Raimond Gaita, *The Philosopher's Dog* (London: Routledge, 2003), p.199.

14. 'Animal Experimentation, Ethics and Medical Research', in Jeremy Stangroom, *What Scientists Think* (London and New York: Routledge, 2005), p.130.

15. Yi-Fu Tuan, *Dominance and Affection* (New Haven: Yale University Press, 1984).

16. M .K. Gewolls and S. M. Labott, 'Adjustment to the Death of a Companion Animal', *Anthrozoös*, 7.3 (1994); L. Stallones, 'Pet Loss and Mental Health', *Anthrozoös*, 7.1 (1994).

17. George Pitcher, *The Dogs who Came to Stay* (New York: Plume, 1996), p.118.

18. Margolies (1999), p.298.

19. For a treatment of 'balanced care', see Michael Slote, *Morals from Motives* (Oxford: Oxford University Press, 2001), chapter 3. Slote does *not* extend this approach to other creatures, but allows that it might be so extended.

Chapter 7

1. Home Office, *Statistics of Scientific Procedures on Living Animals, 2007* (London: The Stationery Office, 2008), Table 1, pp.16–17.

2. Arnold Arluke, '"We Build a Better Beagle": Fantastic Creatures in Lab Animal Ads', *Qualitative Sociology*, 17.2 (1994), pp.143–58; Arnold B. Arluke, 'Sacrificial Symbolism in Animal Experimentation: Object or Pet?', *Anthrozoös*, 2.2 (1988), pp.98–117.

3. http://www.abc.net.au/news/stories/2010/01/16/2793887.htm.

4. 'Gene Function in Tumorigenesis'; 'The Assessment of Biocompatibility'; 'Respiratory Pathogen Induced Inflammation'; 'Smooth Muscle Structure and Contractility'; 'Functional Organisation of the Basal Ganglia'; 'Developing New treatments for Leukaemia', http://scienceandresearch. homeoffice.gov.uk/animal-research/publications-and-reference/ 001-abstracts/abstractsfrom2009/february2009/.

5. Home Office (2008), pp.5, 11.

6. Judith Shklar, *Ordinary Vices* (Cambridge MA: Harvard University Press, 1984), pp.30–5.

7. Steve Jones, 'View From the Lab', *The Daily Telegraph*, 25 March 2009.

8. Home Office (2008), Table 1a, pp.18–19.

9. For a link to some useful US data tables http://www.all-creatures.org/ saen/res-usda-anexstats.html.

10. http://www.nuffieldbioethics.org/fileLibrary/pdf/RIA_Report_ FINAL-opt.pdf.
11. Marcus (2005), p.5.
12. Pandora Pound et al. 'Where Is the Evidence that Animal Research Benefits Humans?', *British Medical Journal*, 328, 514–17, 2 May 2009.
13. Home Office (2008), Table 1, pp.16–17; Table 1a, pp.18–19.
14. Jones (2009).
15. Blakemore interview, Stangroom (2005), p.130.
16. For the moral significance of bonding, see chapter 6 on pets.
17. Blakemore interview, Stangroom (2005), pp.130–1.
18. Stephen R. L. Clark, 'The Rights of Wild Things', in Clark, *Animals and Their Moral Standing* (London and New York: Routledge, 1997), pp.25–7.
19. Charles Darwin (2004), chapter 22.
20. The C. S. Lewis novels that I draw these scenarios from are *Out of the Silent Planet* and *That Hideous Strength*.
21. Shklar (1984), chapter 1.
22. Home Office (2008), p.6.

Bibliography

Arluke, Arnold B. (1988), 'Sacrificial symbolism in animal experimentation: Object or pet?', *Anthrozoös*, 2.2, 98–117.

Arluke, Arnold B. (1994), '"We build a better beagle": Fantastic creatures in lab animal ads', *Qualitative Sociology*, 17.2, 143–58.

Bakhtin, Mikhail (1993), *Rabelais and His World*, Bloomington: Indiana University Press.

Barnard, T., Kramer, S. (2008), *How it all Vegan*, London: Grub Street.

Budiansky, Stephen (1997), *The Covenant of the Wild*, London: Phoenix.

Carson, Rachel (2000), *Silent Spring*, London: Penguin.

Clark, Stephen, R. L. (1997), *Animals and Their Moral Standing*, London and New York: Routledge.

Coetzee, J. M. (2004), *Elizabeth Costello*, London: Vintage.

Cohen, Andrew I. (2007), 'Contractarianism. Other-regarding attitudes, and the moral standing of nonhuman animals', *Journal of Applied Philosophy*, 24.2, 188–201.

Corliss, Richard (2002), 'Should we all be vegetarians?', *Time*, July 15.

Darwin, Charles (2004), *The Descent of Man*, London: Penguin.

Davis, Steven (2003), 'The least harm principal may require that humans consume a diet containing large herbivores, not a vegan diet', *Journal of Agricultural and Environmental Ethics*, 16, 387–94.

Dawkins M. S., Bonney, R. (2008), *The Future of Animal Farming*, Oxford: Blackwell.

Diamond, Cora (1991), *The Realistic Spirit*, Cambridge, MA: MIT Press.

Douglas, Mary (2002), *Purity and Danger*, London and New York: Routledge.

Eshel, G., Martin, P (2006), 'Diet, energy and global warming', *Earth Interactions*, 10, 1–17.

Evans Prichard, E. E. (1940), *The Nuer: A Description of the Modes of Livelihood and Political Institution of a Nilotic People*, Oxford: Oxford University Press.

Fearnley-Whittingstall, Hugh (2004), *The River Cottage Meat Book*, London: Hodder & Stoughton.

Francione, Gary (2008), *Animals as Persons: Essays on the Abolition of Animal Exploitation*, New York: Columbia University Press.

Gaita, Raimond (2003), *The Philosopher's Dog*, London: Routledge.

Gaita, Raimond (2004), *Good and Evil: An Absolute Conception*, London: Routledge.

Garvey, James (2008), *The Ethics of Climate Change*, London: Continuum.

Gewolls, M. K., Labott, S. M. (1994), 'Adjustment to the death of a companion animal', *Anthrozoos*, 7.3, 172–87.

Grandin, Temple (2009), *Animals Make us Human*, New York: Houghton-Mifflin Harcourt.

Guthman, Julie (2004), *Agrarian Dreams*, California: University of California Press.

Haddad, E. H., Tanzman, S. J. (2003), 'What do vegetarians in the United States eat?' *American Journal of Clinical Nutrition*, 78, 626S–632S.

Home Office (2008), *Statistics of Scientific Procedures on Living Animals, 2007*, London: The Stationery Office.

Jones, Steve (2009), 'View from the Lab', *The Daily Telegraph*, 25 March.

Kant, Immanuel (1997), *Lectures on Ethics*, Cambridge: Cambridge University Press.

Kingsolver, Barbara (2007), *Animal, Vegetable, Miracle*, London: Faber and Faber.

Larrère, C., Larrère, R. (2000), 'Animal rearing as a contract', *Journal of Agricultural and Animal Ethics*, 12.1, 51–8.

Law, Stephen (2001), *The Philosophy Files*, London: Dolphin.

Law, Stephen (2003), *The Philosopher's Gym*, London: St Martin's Press.

Leopold, Aldo (1968), *A Sand Country Almanac*, Oxford: Oxford University Press.

Lovelock, James (2007), *The Revenge of Gaia*, London: Penguin.

Maimonides, Moses (2004), *A Guide for the Perplexed*, 4th edition, New York: E.P. Dutton.

Marcus, Erik (2005), *Meat Market*, Boston: Brio.

Margolies, Liz (1999), 'The long good-bye: Women, companion animals, and maternal loss', *Clinical Social Work Journal*, 27.3, 289–304.

Matheny, Gaverick (2003), 'Least harm: A defence of vegetarianism from Steve Davis' Omnivorous Proposal', *Journal of Agricultural and Environmental Ethics*, 16, 501–11.

Matheny, G., Chan, K. (2005), 'Human diets and animal welfare: The illogic of the larder', *Journal of Agricultural and Environmental Ethics*, 18, 579–94.

McSmith, Andy (2009), 'Marcus the sheep falls Victim to ruthless primary school pupils', *The Independent*, 12 September.

Messina, V., Mangels, A. (2001), 'Considerations in planning vegan diets: Children', *Journal of the American Dietetic Association*, 101, 661–69.

Midgley, Mary (1983), *Animals and Why They Matter*, Athens: University of Georgia Press.

Milligan, Tony (2009), 'Dependent Companions', *Journal of Applied Philosophy*, 26.4, 402–13.

Myers, Adrien (2005), *Organic Futures: The Case for Organic Farming*, Devon: Green Books.

Nussbaum, Martha (2001), *Upheavals of Thought*, New York: Cambridge University Press.

O'Connell, J. M., Dibley, M. J., Sierra, J., Wallace, B., Marks, J. S., Yip, R. (1989), 'Growth of vegetarian children: The farm study', *Paediatrics*, 84, 475–81.

Osborne, Catherine (2007), *Dumb Beasts and Dead Philosophers*, Oxford: Oxford University Press.

Parfit, Derek (1984), *Reasons and Persons*, Oxford: Oxford University Press.

Pearson, Louisa (2009), 'As muck would have it', *Scotland on Sunday*, 15 November.

Pimentel, D., Pimentel, M (2003), 'Sustainability of meat-based and plant-based diets and the environment', *American Journal of Clinical Nutrition*, 78, 660S–663S.

Pitcher, George (1996), *The Dogs who Came to Stay*, New York: Plume.

Plutarch (1957), 'On the Eating of Flesh' in Plutarch, *Moralia*, Cambridge, MA: Harvard University Press, volume 12, 537–79.

Pollan, Michael (2001), 'The organic-industrial complex', *New York Times Magazine*, 13 May.

Pollan, Michael (2006), *The Omnivore's Dilemma*, New York: Penguin.

Pollan, Michael (2009), *In Defence of Food*, London: Penguin.

Pound, P., Ebrahim, S., Sandercock, P., Bracken, M. B., Roberts, I. (2009), 'Where is the evidence that animal research benefits humans?', *British Medical Journal*, 328, 2 May, 514–17.

Proust, Marcel (2002), *In Search of Lost Time*, London: Vintage.

Rawls, John (1971), *A Theory of Justice*, Cambridge, MA: Harvard University Press.

Regan, T. and Singer, P. (1976), *Animal Rights and Human Obligations*, New Jersey: Prentice-Hall.

Rollin, Bernard, E. (1995), *The Frankenstein Syndrome: Ethical and Social Issues in the Genetic Engineering of Animals*, New York: Cambridge University Press.

Sanders, T. A. B., Reddy, S. (1994), 'Vegetarian diets and children', *American Journal of Clinical Nutrition*, 59, 1176S–1181S.

Scruton, Roger (2000), *Animal Rights and Wrongs*, 3rd edition, London: Metro Books.

Shafer-Landau, Russ (2003), *Moral Realism: A Defence*, Oxford: Oxford University Press.

Shklar, Judith (1984), *Ordinary Vices*, Cambridge, MA: Harvard University Press.

Singer, Peter (1993), *Practical Ethics*, 2nd edition, New York: Cambridge University Press.

Singer, Peter (1995), *Animal Liberation*, 2nd edition, London: Pimlico.

Singer, P., Mason, J. (2006), *Eating: What We Eat and Why it Matters*, London: Arrow.

Slote, Michael (2001), *Morals from Motives*, Oxford: Oxford University Press.

Stallones, L. (1994), 'Pet loss and mental health', *Anthrozoos*, 7.1, 43–54.

Stangroom, Jeremy (2005), *What Scientists Think*, London and New York: Routledge.

Steinfeld, H., Gerber, P., Wassenaar, T., Castel, V., Rosales, M., de Haan, C. (2006), *Livestock's Long Shadow*, Rome: FAO.

Stephen, Leslie (1896), *Social Rights and Duties*, volume 1, London: Swan Sonnenshein & Co. Ltd.

Telfer, Elizabeth (1996), *Food for Thought*, London and New York: Routledge.

Thane, C. W., Bates, C. J. (2000), 'Dietary intake and nutrient status of vegetarian pre-school children from a British national survey', *Journal of Human Nutrition and Dietetics*,13.6, 149–62.

Tuan, Yi-Fu (1984), *Dominance and Affection*, New Haven: Yale University Press.

Tudge, Colin (2003), *So Shall We Reap*, London: Penguin.

Tyson Foods (2005), *Tyson Foods Investor Factbook* (Tyson Foods, Inc.).

Vegan Society (2008), *Animal Free Shopper*, 8th edition, Birmingham: The Vegan Society.

Velleman, J. David (1999), 'Love as a moral emotion', *Ethics*, 109, 338–74.

Warren, Karen (1990), 'The power and promise of ecological feminism', *Environmental Ethics*, 12.2, 125–46.

Willis, Judith (2008), *The Green Food Bible*, London: Eden Project Books.

Index